THE THAI SYSTEM
OF WRITING

Mary R. Haas

About the Author

David S. Tatel served on the United States Court of Appeals for the District of Columbia Circuit from 1994 to 2024. Prior to that, his three-decade career as a civil rights lawyer focused heavily on equal educational opportunity, voting rights, and access to justice. He was the founding director of the Chicago Lawyers' Committee for Civil Rights Under Law and then director of the National Lawyers' Committee. He headed the Office for Civil Rights of the US Department of Health, Education, and Welfare during the Carter administration and then founded and led the education practice at Hogan Lovells, where he is now Senior Counsel. Judge Tatel, his wife, Edie, and his guide dog, Vixen, live in Virginia and Washington, D.C. They have four children, eight grandchildren, and one great-grandchild.

THE THAI SYSTEM OF WRITING

Mary R. Haas

Spoken Language Services, Inc.

AMERICAN COUNCIL OF LEARNED SOCIETIES

Program in Oriental Languages

Publication Series B — Aids — Number 5

The research and compilation of which this work is a result
were brought to completion under a subvention from the
Board on Overseas Training and Research (Ford Foundation)

ISBN
0-87950-266-5

Library of Congress Number
55-3219

P R E F A C E

In 1942 a small volume entitled "The Thai System
of Writing" was prepared by the author. Reproduced
by the Ditto process, it was used in Thai classes
at the University of Michigan and later at the University of California, Berkeley. The present volume
is a completely revised and rewritten version of that
earlier work.

This book is designed to be used in conjunction
with two other recently published books, namely the
THAI READER and the THAI VOCABULARY (American Council of Learned Societies, 1954 and 1955). All words
cited in the present book are followed by a phonetic
transcription (see Phonetic Key and Charts on the
pages immediately following this preface). This is
necessary so that all phases of the writing system,
both regular and irregular, will be entirely clear
even to the student who wishes to learn the system
by self-study. Before he can learn to read Thai ef-
fectively, however, the student will need to rid
himself entirely of any tendency to "lean" on the
phonetic transcription. This can probably be best
accomplished by the method described in the following paragraphs.

Unlike the previous edition of this book the present book has no exercises. However, this lack can
be adequately compensated for if the student will
make full use of the materials provided in this book
and in the THAI READER. The author recommends the

following procedures:

(1) As soon as the student has covered the material in the first 22 pages of this book he can turn back to the examples beginning on p. 19 and practice reading them without the aid of the phonetic transcription by placing a blank sheet of paper over the transcriptions.

(2) After the student has learned the basic rules of the Thai writing system (i.e. has covered the material in the first three chapters, pp. 1-40), he is ready to begin the study of the THAI READER. Before attempting to read any full phrases or sentences, the student should first study the vocabulary of each lesson in the READER, then review and check his ability to read the individual words in that vocabulary by covering the phonetic transcriptions with a blank sheet of paper. For best results practice reading the words aloud.

(3) As he progresses to the more advanced chapters of the THAI SYSTEM OF WRITING, the student should continue to review each section and chapter by covering the phonetic transcriptions with a blank sheet of paper and reading the examples aloud.

(4) Similarly, as he proceeds to the more advanced lessons in the THAI READER, he should continue to check and review each vocabulary by covering the phonetic transcriptions and reading the examples aloud.

(5) The student should also memorize at least some of the lessons in the THAI READER. This device is particularly useful in the early stages of the study of the Thai writing system.

Most of the Thai words and phrases in this book
are shown in typewritten form. The first time any
symbols are introduced to the reader, however, they
are shown as large-sized handdrawn symbols; see
pp. 6-9, consonants; pp. 15 and 18, vowels; p. 17,
tonal markers; and p. 83, numerals. Over and above
this a few samples of handwriting are also included
in the book (pp. 104-107).

Grateful acknowledgement is made to the American
Council of Learned Societies for support in the production of the original version of this work and for
their assistance in the publication of the present
revised work. I am also deeply grateful to Mr. Heng
R. Subhanka who first taught me how to read and
write Thai and who gave me many valuable suggestions
about the arrangement of presentation in the original version. Many of his suggestions have been retained in the present work. Mr. Sobhak Kasemsanta
has provided the large handdrawn samples of Thai
writing symbols. Samples of Thai handwriting in
three different styles were written out by Miss Pun-
nee Kiangsiri (pp. 104-105). Mr. Waiwit Buddhari
provided the other two samples of Thai handwriting
(pp. 106-107) and also assisted in the proofreading.
Mr. George V. Grekoff drew in the lines in various
charts which are interspersed in the beginning sections of the book.

MARY R. HAAS

University of California, Berkeley
November, 1955

PHONETIC KEY AND CHARTS

Consonants

Note. Consonants followed by a hyphen occur only in initial position; the one preceded by a hyphen only in final position. The rest occur in both positions.

/ʔ/   The glottal stop.

/b/   Voiced unaspirated bilabial stop. In initial position like Eng. b in bid. In final position like Eng. b in crib, but unreleased.

/c-/   Voiceless unaspirated palatal stop. Similar to Eng. ch in chin but without the aspiration that accompanies the Eng. sound.

/ch-/   Voiceless aspirated palatal stop. Similar to Eng. ch in chin but with stronger aspiration.

/d/   Voiced unaspirated postdental stop. In initial position like Eng. d in day. In final position like Eng. d in red, but unreleased.

/f-/   Voiceless labiodental spirant. Like Eng. f in fame. (Occurs rarely in final position in a few recent loan-words from Eng.)

/-g/   Voiced unaspirated velar stop. Only in final position and like Eng. g in big, but unreleased.

/h-/   Voiceless aspirate. Like Eng. h in hat.

/j/   Voiced palatal semivowel. Like Eng. y in you.

/k-/   Voiceless unaspirated velar stop. Like Eng. k in key but without the aspiration that accompanies the Eng. sound. Hence more like French or Italian "hard" c (i.e. k/, as in Fr. café.

/kh-/   Voiceless aspirated velar stop. Like Eng. k in key but with stronger aspiration.

/l-/   Voiced lateral. Like l in Eng. look. (Occurs rarely in final position in a few recent loanwords from English.)

/m/   Voiced bilabial nasal. Like Eng. m in make, come.

/n/   Voiced postdental nasal. Like Eng. n in now, win.

/ŋ/   Voiced velar nasal. Like Eng. ng in song, but in Thai the sound occurs in initial as well as final position.

/p-/   Voiceless unaspirated bilabial stop. Like Eng. p in pin but without the aspiration. Compare Fr. or Ital. p.

/ph-/   Voiceless aspirated bilabial stop. Like Eng. p in pin but with stronger aspiration.

/r-/   Voiced retroflex or weak trill. Compare Eng. r in red.

/s-/   Voiceless sibilant. Like Eng. s in sun. (Occurs rarely in final position in a few loanwords.)

/t-/   Voiceless unaspirated postdental stop. Like Eng. t in ten but without the aspiration. Compare Fr. or Ital. t.

/th-/   Voiceless aspirated postdental stop. Like Eng. t in ten but with stronger aspiration.

/w/   Voiced bilabial semivowel. Like Eng. w in walk, how, but with greater friction and more lip rounding.

Vowels

/a/, /aa/   Low central vowels. Like Eng. a in father. /a/, short; /aa/, long.

/e/, /ee/   Mid front vowels. Like Eng. e in hen. /e/, short; /ee/, long.

/ɛ/, /ɛɛ/   Low front vowels. Like Eng. a in cat. /ɛ/, short; /ɛɛ/, long.

/ə/, /əə/   Mid central vowels. Similar to Eng. er in her but, as in British Eng., without the final r. /ə/, short; /əə/, long.

/i/, /ii/   High front vowels. Like Eng. <u>ee</u> in <u>meek</u>. /i/, short; /ii/, long.

/ia/   /i/ plus /a/ without any pause or break between.

/o/, /oo/   Mid back rounded vowels. Like Eng. <u>o</u> in <u>lone</u>. /o/, short; /oo/, long.

/ɔ/, /ɔɔ/   Low back rounded vowels. Like Eng. <u>o</u> in <u>song</u> or <u>aw</u> in <u>law</u>. /ɔ/, short; /ɔɔ/, long.

/u/, /uu/   High back rounded vowels. Like Eng. <u>oo</u> in <u>noon</u>. /u/; short; /uu/, long.

/ua/   /u/ plus /a/ without any pause or break between.

/y/, /yy/   High central unrounded vowels. Made by raising the center part of the tongue while keeping the lips in relaxed or protracted position. /y/, short; /yy/, long.

/ya/   /y/ plus /a/ without any pause or break between.

Tones

/ˋ/   Low tone. Pitched at a comfortable low range of the voice. The pitch and contour of the remaining tones are described below in relation to the low tone.

/ˇ/   Rising tone. Rises from the pitch of the low tone to the pitch of the high tone.

/ˊ/   High tone. About a fifth above the low tone. At phrase end has glottal stricture and a quick drop.

/ˆ/   Falling tone. Falls from the pitch of the high tone to that of the low tone. At phrase end has glottal stricture.

/ /   (Absence of a mark.) Middle tone. Pitch approximately a major second above the low tone. At phrase end has a very slight drop.

CONSONANT CHART

	Bila-bial	Post-dental	Pala-tal	Velar	Glot-tal
STOPS					
Vd.Unaspirated	b	d		-g	
Vl.Unaspirated	p-	t-	c-	k-	ʔ
Vl.Aspirated	ph-	th-	ch-	kh-	
SPIRANTS					
Vl.Unaspirated	f-	s-			h-
SONORANTS					
Vd.Semivowels	w		j		
Vd.Nasals	m	n		ŋ	
Vd.Lateral		l-			
Vd.Trill (or Retroflex)		r-			

VOWEL CHART

	Front Unrounded	Central Unrounded	Back Rounded
High	i, ii, ia	y, yy, ya	u, uu, ua
Mid	e, ee	ɘ, ɘɘ	o, oo
Low	ɛ, ɛɛ	a, aa	ɔ, ɔɔ

TONE CONTOURS IN ISOLATION

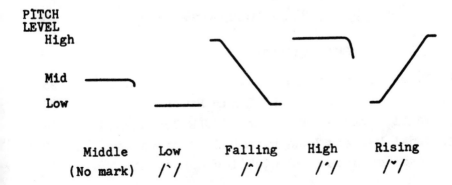

Middle (No mark)	Low /ˋ/	Falling /ˆ/	High /ˊ/	Rising /ˇ/

TABLE OF CONTENTS

INTRODUCTION

The Thai system of writing is one of many varieties of the Devanagari writing system which have
spread out from India. The immediate source is the
Cambodian variety. To this day the Thai numerals
and the Cambodian numerals are identical, but the
alphabetical symbols, while similar, are sufficiently diverse so that each system must be learned
separately.

The particular adaptation of the Thai alphabet
as a separate system of writing was devised by (or
at the request of) Ramkhamhaeng the Great of Sukho-
thai. The first written monument, an engraved block
of stone known as the Inscription of King Ramkhamhaeng, is assigned to the year 1283 A.D. [See
Cornelius B. Bradley, "The oldest known writing in
Siamese," Journal of the Siam Society, vol. 6,
pt. 1 (1909), pp. 1-64.]

The modern Thai writing system is directly descend-
ed from the form of writing preserved in this earli-
est inscription, though certain changes (which need
not concern us here) have been introduced since that
time. Another slightly different derivative of that
early form of writing is the system used by the Lao
(Laotians) of the Kingdom of Laos which lies to the
northeast of Thailand.

The language spoken by the authors of the inscription was similar to the modern standard dialect of
Bangkok, but certain features still preserved in the
modern writing system show us that it was not identical at all points.

1

The description of the Thai system of writing
which is provided in the present volume gives the
pronunciation entirely in terms of the modern standard dialect of Bangkok. In addition to the standard
dialect there are three other major dialects spoken
within the boundaries of the nation, viz. the South-
ern, the Northern and the Northeastern. The Northern
dialect had at one time its own special system of
writing, but this is now virtually obsolete. At the
present time, if the Northern dialect is written at
all, it is written by using the letters of the
standard system. The Northeastern dialect was formerly written in a system like that used by the Lao,
mentioned above, but this too is now largely obsolete within the boundaries of Thailand.

At the present time the standard dialect of Bangkok together with the standard writing system used
for that dialect is the literary medium taught in
all the schools throughout the nation.

CHAPTER I

T H.E T H A I C O N S O N A N T S A N D
T H E I R N A M E S

1. General Remarks

The Thai system of writing, as a derivative of
the Devanagari system, has retained the basic sequence of arrangement for consonants found in the
Indic system. This sequence of arrangement consti-
tutes the alphabetical order used in standard Thai
dictionaries and must be memorized for an efficient
use of such dictionaries. There are the following
six major groups of consonants:

1. Velars
2. Palatals
3. Retroflexes (pronounced as dentals in Thai)
4. Dentals
5. Labials
6. Miscellaneous (the remaining sonorants and
   spirants and the glottal stop)

Because of historical changes that have taken place
in the pronunciation of some of the consonants, not
all of them are now pronounced in accordance with
what we might expect from their position in the total sequence; but the deviations are relatively few
and the reasons for them need not concern us here.

Within each of the first five of the major groups
listed above the sequence shown on the following
page is observed where pertinent. The sequence con-
sists in five major categories based on phonetic
criteria.

1. A. <u>Voiced</u> <u>stop</u>. MIDDLE (see Comment on p. 5).
   Lacking in the velar and the palatal groups.
   B. <u>Voiceless</u> <u>unaspirated</u> <u>stop</u>. MIDDLE.

2. A. <u>Voiceless</u> <u>aspirated</u> <u>stop</u> with inherent <u>rising</u>
   tone. HIGH. In the velar group there are two
   consonants coming in this category but the
   second of the two is now obsolete.
   B. <u>Voiceless</u> <u>spirant</u> with inherent <u>rising</u> tone.
   HIGH. In the labial group only.

3. A. <u>Voiceless</u> <u>aspirated</u> <u>stop</u> with inherent <u>middle</u>
   tone. LOW. In the velar group there are three
   consonants coming in this category but the second of the two is now obsolete. The third one
   is described under 4 below.
   B. <u>Voiceless</u> <u>spirant</u> with inherent <u>middle</u> tone.
   LOW. In the labial group only.

4. <u>Voiceless</u> <u>aspirated</u> <u>stop</u> with inherent <u>middle</u>
   tone. LOW. Used to transcribe Sanskrit or Pali
   voiced aspirated stops.

5. <u>Voiced</u> <u>nasal</u>. LOW. In the standard dialect of
   Bangkok the nasal symbol of the palatal group is
   pronounced /j/ in initial position, /n/ in final
   position. In some provincial dialects the palatal nasal is pronounced as such, viz. /ñ/.

The complete list of the 44 consonants of the
Thai alphabet is given on pp. 6-9. Of these the 3rd
and 5th are obsolete, having been replaced by the
2nd and 4th, respectively. Standard Thai dictionaries and books on the alphabet still list all 44 consonants for the sake of completeness.

Each consonant letter is pronounced with the carrying vowel /-ɔɔ/. The consonant <u>sound</u> preceding the

/-ɔɔ/ is the phonetic value of that letter in syllable-initial position. Thus the letter ก /kɔɔ/ has
the sound /k-/ in syllable-initial position. Many
consonants have a different phonetic value when they
occur in syllable-final position. This is shown in
charts on pp. 54 and 58.

There is also an inherent tone belonging to each
consonant letter. This is either the <u>middle</u> tone,
as in /kɔɔ/, the 1st letter, or the <u>rising</u> tone, as
in /khˇɔɔ/, the 2nd letter. This tone must be memorized as an integral part of the name of each consonant. See the comment below.

> <u>Comment</u>. Thai consonants are divided into
> three major tonal classes known as MIDDLE, HIGH,
> and LOW. The constituent members of each of these
> classes are listed and discussed on pp. 10-13.
> All spelling rules having to do with the indica-
> tion of tones are determined by this three-way
> classification. The inherent tone of all MIDDLE
> and all LOW consonants is the <u>middle</u> tone, e.g.
> /kɔɔ/, the 1st letter and a MIDDLE consonant;
> /khɔɔ/, the 4th letter and a LOW consonant. The
> inherent tone of all HIGH consonants is the
> <u>rising</u> tone, e.g. /khˇɔɔ/, the 2nd letter and a
> HIGH consonant.

Each consonant letter has also been provided with
an arbitrary designatory name to be used when spelling words orally. This arbitrary name is usually
some common noun spelled with the letter so desig-
nated, e.g. /kɔɔ kàj/ "<u>kɔɔ</u> chicken." Rarer consonant letters, however, have often been given names
referring to entities which are somewhat less famil-
iar. Thai children learn to recite the alphabet by
using these designatory names.

6

2. List of Consonants

Symbol	Thai Name	Transcription and Meaning

V E L A R S

ก	ก ไก่	/kɔɔ kàj/ chicken
ข	ข ไข่	/khɔ̌ɔ khàj/ egg
ฃ	ฃ ขวด	/khɔ̌ɔ khùad/ bottle [Obsolete] Replaced by letter #2 above.
ค	ค ควาย	/khɔɔ khwaaj/ water buffalo
ฅ	ฅ คน	/khɔɔ khon/ person [Obsolete] Replaced by letter #4 above.
ฆ	ฆ ระฆัง	/khɔɔ rákhaŋ/ bell
ง	ง งู	/ŋɔɔ ŋuu/ snake

P A L A T A L S

จ	จ จาน	/cɔɔ caan/ plate
ฉ	ฉ ฉิ่ง	/chɔ̌ɔ chìŋ/ cymbal
ช	ช ช้าง	/chɔɔ cháaŋ/ elephant
ซ	ซ โซ่	/sɔɔ sôo/ chain
ฌ	ฌ กะเฌอ	/chɔɔ kàchəə/ tree (Camb.)
ญ	ญ หญิง	/jɔɔ jǐŋ/ woman

Symbol	Thai Name	Transcription and Meaning

R E T R O F L E X E S (PRONOUNCED AS DENTALS)

Symbol	Thai Name	Transcription and Meaning
ฏ	ฏ ชฎา	/dɔɔ chádaa/ tall headgear worn by actors
ฏ	ฏ ปฏัก	/tɔɔ pàtàg/ (a) goad
ฐ	ฐ ฐาน	/thɔ̌ɔ thǎan/ base, pedestal
ฑ	ฑ นางมณโฑ	/thɔɔ naaŋmonthoo/ name of a giant's wife in Ramayana epic
ฒ	ฒ ผู้เฒ่า	/thɔɔ phûuthâw/ old person
ณ	ณ เณร	/nɔɔ neen/ young Buddhist disciple

D E N T A L S

Symbol	Thai Name	Transcription and Meaning
ด	ด เด็ก	/dɔɔ dèg/ child
ต	ต เต่า	/tɔɔ tàw/ turtle
ถ	ถ ถุง	/thɔ̌ɔ thǔŋ/ sack, bag
ท	ท ทหาร	/thɔɔ tháhǎan/ soldier
ธ	ธ ธง	/thɔɔ thoŋ/ flag, emblem
น	น หนู	/nɔɔ nǔu/ mouse, rat

Symbol	Thai Name	Transcription and Meaning

L A B I A L S

บ	บ ใบไม้	/bɔɔ bajmáaj/ leaf
ป	ป ปลา	/pɔɔ plaa/ fish
ผ	ผ ผึ้ง	/phɔɔ phŷŋ/ bee
ฝ	ฝ ฝา	/fɔɔ fǎa/ lid, cover
พ	พ พาน	/phɔɔ phaan/ tray with ped- estal base
ฟ	ฟ ฟัน	/fɔɔ fan/ tooth, teeth
ภ	ภ สำเภา	/phɔɔ sǎmphaw/ a kind of sail boat, junk
ม	ม ม้า	/mɔɔ máa/ horse

M I S C E L L A N E O U S

ย	ย ยักษ์	/jɔɔ ják/ giant
ร	ร เรือ	/rɔɔ rya/ boat, ship
ล	ล ลิง	/lɔɔ liŋ/ monkey
ว	ว แหวน	/wɔɔ wěɛn/ fingerring
ศ	ศ ศาลา	/sɔɔ sǎalaa/ pavilion
ษ	ษ ฤาษี	/sɔɔ ryysǐi/ hermit, anchor- ite
ส	ส เสือ	/sɔɔ sỹa/ tiger

Symbol	Thai Name	Transcription and Meaning

M I S C E L L A N E O U S (CONTINUED)

Symbol	Thai Name	Transcription and Meaning
ห	ห หีบ	/hɔ̌ɔ hìib/ box
ฬ	ฬ จุฬา	/lɔɔ cùlaa/ a kind of kite
อ	อ อ่าง	/ʔɔɔ ʔàaŋ/ basin
ฮ	ฮ นกฮูก	/hɔɔ nóghûug/ owl

~~~~~~

HOW TO MAKE THE CONSONANT SYMBOLS

All consonants except ก /kɔɔ kàj/ and ธ /thɔɔ thoŋ/ are started with the production of their characteristic little CIRCLE. If there is more than one little circle start with the one on the left. The pen then moves up or down, to the right or the left, as required. It is very important to note whether the circle is to the RIGHT or to the LEFT of its connecting line. This is the only difference between ค and ด, and between ถ and ภ, i.e. between /khɔɔ khwaaj/ and /dɔɔ dèg/ and between /thɔ̌ɔ thǔŋ/ and /phɔɔ sǎmphaw/, and others.

The symbol ก is made in two strokes. The left-hand line starts just under the "roof" and is made as a downward stoke. The second stroke starts at the same point, then moves around to the right and down. ธ starts with a similar downward stroke but continues without the pen being lifted.

IF THE STUDENT WILL USE TRACING PAPER AND FIRST PRACTICE BY TRACING OVER THE LARGE SYMBOLS SHOWN ON PAGES 6-9 HE WILL SOON BE ABLE TO DO THEM FREEHAND.

3. The Three Classes of Consonants

Thai consonants are divided into three major
tonal classes known as MIDDLE, HIGH, and LOW. The
constituent members of these classes are shown on
pp. 11-13. These must be memorized because the tonal markers (Chap. III, p. 25) used to indicate the
tones have different values depending upon the
class of the consonant with which they are being
used. Within each class of consonants there are
some which are used less frequently than others.
This information is included in connection with the
discussion of each of the three classes. It will
prove useful to the student who wishes to learn to
spell as rapidly as possible. See comment below.

Comment. It frequently happens that the same
consonant sound of the Thai language is written
by two or more different consonant letters. If
the two or more consonant letters belong to different consonant classes there is no conflict.
The tone of the syllable usually determines the
class of the letter to be used. Thus with but
one exception (described on p. 35) there is no
conflict between /khɔ̌ɔ khàj/, a HIGH consonant,
and /khɔɔ khwaaj/, a LOW consonant.

On the other hand, if two or more consonant
sounds can be written with consonant letters belonging to the same class, a conflict arises. In
such a case the choice of consonant letter is determined solely by the dictates of the rules of
correct spelling. Thus there is a conflict between
/khɔɔ khwaaj/, a LOW consonant, and /khɔɔ rákhaŋ/,
another LOW consonant. But even here it is possible to make a general statement which will be of
great help to the student. Most words beginning

with the /kh-/ sound and having a tone which must
be written with a LOW consonant are spelled with
/khɔɔ khwaaj/. Hence the student need only memorize those few words which must be spelled with
/khɔɔ rákhaŋ/. He can easily remember that all
the rest are spelled with /khɔɔ khwaaj/ whenever
a LOW consonant is required.

MIDDLE CONSONANTS

There are nine MIDDLE consonants and they are
pronounced with inherent <u>middle</u> tone on the carrying vowel /-ɔɔ/. They comprise all of the consonant symbols standing for <u>voiced stops</u> and <u>voiceless
unaspirated stops</u> as shown below.

Voiced Stops			(ฎ) ด	บ		
Vl.Unasp. Stops	ก	จ	(ฏ) ต	ป	อ	

<u>Comment 1</u>. Conflicting symbols are boxed
together and the rarer symbol is placed in parentheses. The retroflexes /dɔɔ chádaa/ and /tɔɔ
pàtàg/ occur in Sanskrit or Pali loanwords. The
spelling of words containing them should be memorized.

<u>Comment 2</u>. Contrary to what is often stated,
the letter อ /ʔɔɔ ʔàaŋ/ is a true consonant in
the Thai writing system and not merely a carrying symbol for vowels. It is a MIDDLE consonant
and the values of the tonal markers used with it
are precisely the same as they are for all the
rest of the MIDDLE consonants.

HIGH CONSONANTS

There are eleven HIGH consonants and they are pronounced with inherent <u>rising</u> tone on the carrying vowel /-ɔɔ/. They comprise the Thai consonant symbols for one set of <u>voiceless aspirated stops</u> and one set of <u>voiceless spirants</u> as shown below.

Aspir. Stops	ข	ฃ	(ฉ) ฌ	ผ
Spirants		(ฝ)(ศ) ส		ฬ	ห

Comment <u>1</u>. Only ten symbols are shown in the chart. The extra one, /khɔɔ khùad/, is obsolete and has been completely replaced by /khɔɔ khàj/. Conflicting symbols are boxed together and the rarer symbol or symbols are placed in parentheses. The remaining symbols are unique.

Comment <u>2</u>. For each HIGH consonant (or set of HIGH consonants identically pronounced) there is a corresponding LOW consonant (or set of LOW consonants identically pronounced). This pairing of HIGH and LOW consonants is shown in a chart on p. 34.

LOW CONSONANTS

The student should memorize all the MIDDLE consonants and all the HIGH consonants. He need then only remember that all of the remaining consonants of the alphabet are LOW consonants. There are in all twenty-four LOW consonants and they are pro-

nounced with inherent <u>middle</u> tone on the carrying
vowel /-ɔɔ/. They comprise two major groups of
sounds:

    (1) a second set of <u>voiceless aspirated stops</u>
and a second set of <u>voiceless spirants</u>, and

    (2) all of the <u>voiced sonorants</u> (nasals, semi-
vowels and liquids). See the chart below.

Vl. Asp. Stops	ค (ฅ)	ช (ฌ)	(ฑ)(ฒ) ท (ธ)	พ (ภ)	
Vl. Spirants		ฑ		ฟ	ฮ
Voiced Sonorants		ย (ญ)		ร	
	ง	↑	(ณ) น	ม	
			(ฬ) ล		
			ว		

    <u>Comment</u>. Only twenty-three symbols are shown
in the chart. The extra one, /khɔɔ khon/, is obsolete and has been completely replaced by the
symbol known as /khɔɔ khwaaj/. Conflicting symbols are boxed together and the rarer symbol or
symbols are placed in parentheses. See also the
list of regular and irregular initial consonants
shown on pp. 41-42.

CHAPTER II

THE VOCALIC SYMBOLS

1. General Remarks

Vocalic symbols are either SIMPLE (composed of one part) or COMPLEX (composed of more than one part). Of the simple vocalic symbols, some are written <u>before</u> the consonant, some <u>after</u> the consonant, some <u>above</u>, some <u>below</u>. But in any case each vowel as a sound is always pronounced AFTER the consonant or consonant cluster which it accompanies.

The complex vocalic symbols are built up of two or more simple vowel and/or consonant symbols. Since the individual parts of a complex often have values which bear little or no relation to the values they have when used as simplexes, the student is urged to MEMORIZE THE COMPLEX SYMBOLS AS UNITS.

Most vocalic symbols occur in pairs of short and long. The last four symbols, however, are unpaired and stand for short /a/ plus /m, j, w/. Other combinations of short vowel plus sonorant and combinations of long vowel plus sonorant present no special difficulty. A chart showing the paired symbols and the four unpaired symbols is given on p. 15. The symbols are presented in their traditional order reading across, e.g. /sàrà? ?à?/, /sàrà? ?aa/, /sàrà? ?ì?/, /sàrà? ?ii/, etc. The word /sàrà?/ means "vowel." MEMORIZE THE VOWEL SYMBOLS IN THE ORDER GIVEN as an aid to the use of Thai dictionaries. The dash in the chart shows the position of the initial consonant.

All the vocalic symbols are shown in the form they take in syllable-final position. Some have other forms, as shown on p. 18.

14

2. Principal Vocalic Symbols (Syllable-Final Form)

SHORT		Thai Name	LONG		Thai Name
−ะ	−ะ	/sàrà? ?à?/	−า	−า	/sàrà? ?aa/
−ิ	−ิ	/sàrà? ?í?/	−ี	−ี	/sàrà? ?ii/
−ึ	−ึ	/sàrà? ?ỳ?/	−ือ	−ือ	/sàrà? ?yy/
−ุ	−ุ	/sàrà? ?ù?/	−ู	−ู	/sàrà? ?uu/
เ−ะ	เ−ะ	/sàrà? ?è?/	เ−	เ−	/sàrà? ?ee/
แ−ะ	แ−ะ	/sàrà? ?ὲ?/	แ−	แ−	/sàrà? ?εε/
โ−ะ	โ−ะ	/sàrà? ?ò?/	โ−	โ−	/sàrà? ?oo/
เ−าะ	เ−าะ	/sàrà? ?ɔ?/	−อ	−อ	/sàrà? ?ɔɔ/
เ−ัวะ	เ−ัวะ	/sàrà? ?ùa?/	−ัว	−ัว	/sàrà? ?ua/
เ−ียะ	เ−ียะ	/sàrà? ?ìa?/	เ−ีย	เ−ีย	/sàrà? ?ia/
เ−ือะ	เ−ือะ	/sàrà? ?ỳa?/	เ−ือ	เ−ือ	/sàrà? ?ya/
เ−อะ	เ−อะ	/sàrà? ?ə̀?/	เ−อ	เ−อ	/sàrà? ?əə/
−ำ	−ำ	/sàrà? ?am/			
ใ−	ใ−	/sàrà? ?aj/			
ไ−	ไ−	/sàrà? ?aj/			
เ−า	เ−า	/sàrà? ?aw/			

In Thai textbooks the symbol for /sàrà? ?yy/ is given as $\overset{\blacktriangleleft}{-}$ instead of $\overset{\blacktriangleleft}{-}$ච. The symbol $\overset{\blacktriangleleft}{-}$ච is shown in the chart above because the vowel is always written thus in syllable-final position. The other form is used when the vowel is followed by a syllable-closing consonant (see p. 18).

There are two symbols for the combined sound /-aj/ and they are pronounced exactly alike in the standard dialect of Bangkok (see Comment below). The first symbol ไ is known as /májmúan/ and the second symbol ใ as /májmálaaj/. There are in all twenty words which must be spelled with ใ, most of them very common words. The complete list is given on p. 68. Almost all other words having the sound /-aj/ are spelled with ไ, but there remain a very few which are spelled in a third way to be described later (see p. 23).

 <u>Comment</u>. At the time the Thai writing system was developed ใ and ไ were NOT pronounced alike. What the phonetic distinction was at that time is not definitely known. There are modern dialects, however, which maintain a distinction between the two types of sounds. In Shan, for example, words which would be spelled with ใ have a vowel cluster /-ay/, i.e. /a/ plus the high central vowel /y/, while words which would be spelled with ไ are pronounced with /-aj/, just as in the Bangkok dialect, e.g.

SHAN	BANGKOK THAI		Meaning
/nay/	ใน	/naj/	in
/phaj/	ไฟ	/faj/	fire

3. The Phonetic Interpretation of

"Short" Vowel Symbols

All of the "short" vowel symbols shown in the
chart on p. 15 are actually pronounced as a short
vowel (or vowel cluster) plus a syllable-closing
consonant. This syllable-closing consonant is
either the glottal stop /ʔ/, as in the first twelve
symbols, or /m, j, w/, as in the last four. A glance
at the chart will reveal the fact that the symbol
—ː, known as /sàrà ʔ ʔàʔ/, is one which has a dual
function. When used alone it stands for /-aʔ/, but
when combined with other symbols it stands for a
syllable-final /-ʔ/ with shortening of the preceding vowel. Hence no short vowel symbol containing —ː
as a component can ever be used to write a short
vowel plus any other consonant. As a result of this
fact, there are special combinatory symbols which
have to be used to cover those situations in which
—ː cannot be used. These are shown in the following
section.

   Comment. The symbols —́ɔ̈ː, ⊢ʊ̈ː, and ⊢ɑ̈ː are
actually "fake" short vowels. They are listed as
such because they contain —ː as a component, but
the true phonetic value of —ː here, as explained
above, is the final glottal stop /-ʔ/.

4. Additional Vocalic Symbols

There are nine additional simple and complex
vowel symbols for use with all syllable-closing consonants except /-ʔ/, as explained above. Five are
for short vowels and the rest are for long vowels or
vowel clusters. In the chart on p. 18 a dash shows
the position to be assumed by the initial consonant,
a diagonal replaces the syllable-closing consonant.

18

Vocalic Symbols Used with Syllable-Closing Cons.

◌ั/	◌ั/	/-a-/ + C. See Comment 1.
◌ั/	◌ั/	/-yy-/ + C
เ◌็/	เ◌็/	/-e-/ + C. See Comment 2.
แ◌็/	แ◌็/	/-ɛ-/ + C
◌/	◌/	/-o-/ + C. ZERO symbol.
◌็อ/	◌็อ/	/-ɔ-/ + C. Rarely used.
เ◌/	เ◌/	/-əə-/ + C except ย.
เ◌ย	เ◌ย	/-əəj/. See Comment 3.
◌ว/	◌ว/	/-ua-/ + C.

~~~~~~

Comment 1. The symbol ◌ั/ used in writing short /-a-/ plus C is called /májhǎnʔaakàad/ "stick turning in the air."

Comment 2. The vowel shortening symbol ◌็ used with /-e-/, /-ɛ-/, and occasionally /-ɔ-/ is called /májtàjkhúu/. It cannot be used if tonal markers are required.

Comment 3. This symbol is actually the long vowel /-ee-/ plus /-j /, but since there is no such phonetic combination in Thai, the written combination can be used for /-əəj/ without ambiguity.

3. Examples of the Vocalic Symbols

The rules for the ways to indicate tones have not yet been given. The reader should therefore reserve all questions about the why of the tonal indications in the phonetic transcriptions below until he has read the chapter on the tonal markers (pp. 25-40). The explanation of the special devices used in the table below is as follows:

F   "final, i.e. not followed by added cons. to be pronounced in the same syllable"

+C   "followed by a syllable-closing consonant"

	Symbol	Example	Transcription
F	–ะ	จะ	/càʔ/ will, shall
+C	◌ั/	วัน	/wan/ day
F	–า	มา	/maa/ to come
+C	Same	จาน	/caan/ plate
F	◌ิ	ติ	/tìʔ/ to criticize
+C	Same	หิน	/hĭn/ stone, rock
F	◌ี	มี	/mii/ to have
+C	Same	ปีน	/piin/ to climb
F	◌ึ	รึ	/rɣ́ʔ/ (Var. form of the interrog. particle)
+C	Same	ดึง	/dɣŋ/ to pull

	Symbol	Example	Transcription
F	-ือ	มือ	/myy/ hand
+C	-ื/	คืน	/khyyn/ night
F	-ุ	จุ	/cù?/ to be stuffed
+C	Same	ถุง	/thǔŋ/ sack, bag
F	-ู	ดู	/duu/ to look
+C	Same	ถูก	/thùug/ to be right
F	เ-ะ	เกะ	/tè?/ to kick
+C	เ-็/	เต็ม	/tem/ to be full
F	เ-	เท	/thee/ to pour
+C	Same	เพลง	/phleeŋ/ song
F	แ-ะ	แอะ	/lɛ́?/ and
+C	แ-็/	แข็ง	/khɛ̌ŋ/ to be hard, firm
F	แ-	แล	/lɛɛ/ to see, watch
+C	Same	แดง	/dɛɛŋ/ to be red
F	โ-ะ	โต๊ะ	/tó?/ table
+C	Zero	ฝน	/fǒn/ rain
F	โ-	โต	/too/ to be big, large
+C	Same	โมง	/mooŋ/ o'clock

	Symbol	Example	Transcription
F	เ–าะ	เกาะ	/kɔ̀ʔ/ island
+C	–็อ/	หร็อก	/rɔ̀g/ (Emphatic particle)
F	–อ	พอ	/phɔɔ/ to be enough
+C	Same	ลอง	/lɔɔŋ/ to try
F	–ัวะ	ผลัวะ	/phlùaʔ/ (onom. for sound of slapping, banging) RARE
F	–ัว	บัว	/bua/ lotus
+C	–ว/	บวม	/buam/ to swell, be swollen
F	เ–ียะ	เกียะ	/dìaʔ/ quick as a flash RARE
F	เ–ีย	เมีย	/mia/ wife
+C	Same	เสียง	/sǐaŋ/ sound, tone, noise
F	เ–ือะ	เอือะ	/ʔ̀yaʔ/ (name of the symbol shown) EXTREMELY RARE
F	เ–ือ	เรือ	/rya/ boat, ship
+C	Same	เรือน	/ryan/ house
F	เ–อะ	เยอะ	/jə́ʔ/ a whole lot
F	เ–อ	เธอ	/thəə/ you (familiar)
+C	เ–ิ/	เดิน	/dəən/ to walk, proceed
+ย	เ–ย	เนย	/nəəj/ butter

	Symbol	Example	Transcription
F	–ำ	คำ	/kham/ word
F	໌ใ–	ใจ	/caj/ heart, spirit (fig.)
F	ไ–	ไป	/paj/ to go
F	เ–า	เอา	/ʔaw/ to take

∿∿∿

Additional remarks concerning the use of the last four symbols are given in the next section.

6. Short and Long Vowels Plus Sonorants

A very few short and long vowel plus sonorant combinations are written by means of special symbols, all of which have already been given. All remaining short and long vowel plus sonorant combinations are written out in full, i.e. one uses the proper +C vowel symbol followed by the appropriate consonant letter. Although two ways of writing /-aj/ have already been learned, two other ways, both of rare occurrence, are found. These, together with selected samples of other vowel plus sonorant combinations, are illustrated on the following pages (pp. 23-24).

W a r n i n g

Two of the most commonly used final sonorants are ย and ว, and in most cases they are to be read as /-j/ and /-w/, respectively. However, they also occur as components of complex vowel symbols already learned (p. 15), and when they are used in this way they are NEVER read as /-j/ and /-w/. To avoid all confusion on this point the student is urged to memorize the following rules:

เ–ียฺ	is ALWAYS read /-ia/.
–ัว	is ALWAYS read /-ua/, NEVER /-aw/.
เ–า	is the ONLY way to write /-aw/.
–วย	is ALWAYS read /-uaj/.

7. Examples of Vowel plus Sonorant Combinations

A. READ WITH FINAL /-j/

Phon. Value	Writing	Example	Transcription
/-aj/	ไ–	ไกล	/klaj/ to be far
/-aj/ RARE	ไ–ย	ไทย	/thaj/ Thai
/-aj/ (20)	ใ–	ใคร	/khraj/ who, anyone
/-aj/ RARE	–ัย	ภัย	/phaj/ danger
/-aaj/	–าย	ขาย	/khǎaj/ to sell
/-uaj/	–วย	สวย	/sǔaj/ to be pretty
/-ɣaj/	เ–ือย	เรื่อย	/rɣ̂aj/ to be continuous
/-əəj/	เ–ย	เคย	/khəəj/ ever
/-uj/	–ฺย	คุย	/khuj/ to chat
/-ooj/	โ–ย	โดย	/dooj/ by, with
/-ɔj/	–็อย	หย็อกหย็อย	/jɔ̀gjɔ̌j/ disheveled
/-ɔɔj/	–อย	ลอย	/lɔɔj/ to float

B. READ WITH FINAL /-w/

Phon. Value	Writing	Example	Transcription
/-aw/	เ–า	เรา	/raw/ we
/-aaw/	–าว	ขาว	/khǎaw/ to be white
/-iaw/	เ–ียว	เขียว	/khǐaw/ to be green
/-iw/	–ิว	หิว	/hǐw/ to be hungry
/-ew/	เ–็ว	เร็ว	/rew/ to be fast
/-eew/	เ–ว	เลว	/leew/ to be bad
/-ɛɛw/	แ–ว	แมว	/mɛɛw/ cat

~~~~~~

C. READ WITH FINAL /-m, -n, -ŋ/

Phon. Value	Writing	Example	Transcription
/-am/	–ำ	ดำ	/dam/ to be black
/-am/ RARE	–ัม	กรัม	/kram/ gram (< Fr.)
/-aam/	–าม	สาม	/sǎam/ three
/-uam/	–วม	สวม	/sǔam/ to put on, wear
/-an/	–ัน	มัน	/man/ fat, oil
/-aan/	–าน	งาน	/ŋaan/ work; ceremony
/-ɔɔn/	–อน	นอน	/nɔɔn/ to lie (down)
/-yan/	เ–ือน	เดือน	/dyan/ moon, month
/-oŋ/	–ง	ลง	/loŋ/ to descend
/-ooŋ/	โ–ง	โกง	/kooŋ/ to be crooked

~~~~~~

Comment. The above is only a small sample of
the combinations with final /-m, -n, -ŋ/, but
most of such combinations are entirely regular.
Irregular ways of writing final /-an/ and /-ɔɔn/
are described and illustrated on pp. 55-56.

CHAPTER III

T H E   T O N A L   M A R K E R S

1. Types of Syllables

There are two main types of syllables in Thai
which must be distinguished in order to understand
the rules for writing the tones. Using the termin-
ology adopted by the Thai themselves, we may call
them "live" syllables and "dead" syllables. Their
characteristics are described below.

(1) Live syllables comprise the following:

A. All syllables ending in a <u>long vowel</u> or in a
<u>vowel cluster</u>, e.g.

กา	/kaa/	crow	หัว	/hǔa/	head
สี	/sǐi/	color	เสือ	/sɣ̌a/	tiger

B. All syllables ending in a <u>sonorant</u>. In the
spoken language this is either a semivowel,
i.e. /-j, -w/, or a nasal, i.e. /-m, -n, -ŋ/.
In the written language it is a semivowel, a
nasal, or a liquid (i.e. sounds which in initial position are pronounced /l-, r-/), but
syllable-final liquids are normally pronounced
/-n/, p. 54. Examples:

ไฟ	/faj/	fire	นำ	/nam/	to lead
ดาว	/daaw/	star	ลม	/lom/	wind
เดียว	/diaw/	single	เมือง	/myaŋ/	town
ศีล	/sǐin/	moral code	ควร	/khuan/	should, ought to

25

(2) Dead syllables comprise the following:

A. All syllables ending in a __short__ __vowel__. In
most cases these are pronounced as a __short__
__vowel__ __plus__ __glottal__ __stop__ (see p. 17 and cf.
paragraph B below). Examples:

  จะ   /cà?/ will   และ /lɛ́?/ and

  เตะ   /tè?/ to kick   เยอะ /jə́?/ a whole
                                               lot

If this short vowel is not in word-final position, the glottal stop may be dropped. Alternate tonal pronunciations are then possible, the first being a spelling and also a
slow speech pronunciation, the second a rapid
speech pronunciation. Syllables of the second
type may be conveniently called "neutralized"
syllables. Examples:

  ทะเล   /thálee/ ~ /thalee/ sea

  บุหรี่   /bùrìi/ ~ /burìi/ cigar, cigarette

B. All syllables ending in a stop consonant, i.e.
a "dead" consonant. In the spoken language
this is always a voiced unreleased stop. In
the written language it may be a voiced stop,
voiceless unaspirated stop, voiceless aspirated stop, or voiceless spirant, but all of
these are normally pronounced as their homor-
ganic voiced stops in syllable-final position;
see pp. 56-58. Examples:

  สิบ   /sìb/ ten   หีบ   /hìib/ box

  รด   /ród/ to water รูป   /rûub/ picture

  รถ   /ród/ car   แปด /pɛ̀ɛd/ eight

  รส   /ród/ taste   มาก /mâag/ much

"Dead" syllables often need to be further distinguished depending on whether they contain a **short** or a **long** **vowel**. This is explained in the following sections.

2. The Tonal Markers and Their Names

All tonal markers are superscripts. They are placed over the initial consonant of the syllable whose tone they mark. But if the syllable begins in a consonant cluster, the tonal marker is placed over the second of the two consonants. And if that syllable already has a superscript vowel, the tonal marker is placed above the vowel.

Symbol		Name	Transcription
ǃ	'	ไม้เอก	/máj²èeg/ "first stick," i.e. 1st tonal marker
			Low or falling tone (see below)
✓	✓	ไม้โท	/májthoo/ 2nd tonal marker
			Falling or high tone (see below)
∾	∩	ไม้ตรี	/májtrii/ 3rd tonal marker
			High tone
+	⁺	ไม้จัตวา	/májcàdtàwaa/ 4th tonal marker
			Rising tone.

The tonal values of these markers depend upon two conditioning factors, (1) the class of the syllable-initial consonant; see pp. 10-13, and (2) the nature of the syllable with which they are used, i.e. whether it is "live" or "dead"; see pp. 25-26. The rules are given in the following sections.

3. Tonal Markers and MIDDLE Consonants

A. Live Syllables

When used with a MIDDLE consonant initiating a **live** syllable the four tonal markers indicate the low, falling, high, and rising tones, respectively. Absence of a marker indicates the middle tone.

MIDDLE CONSONANT WITH LIVE SYLLABLE

Marker	Value	Example	Transcription
(none)	Middle	ปา	/paa/ to toss
่ —	Low	ป่า	/p̀aa/ forest
้ —	Falling	ป้า	/p̂aa/ elder aunt
*	*	*	* * * * *
๊ —	High	เก๊	/kée/ to be counterfeit (< Chinese)
๋ —	Rising	เก๋	/kěe/ to be chic (< Chin.)
		จ๋า	/cǎa/ yes? (ans. when called--intimate)

∿∿∿

N o r m a l   a n d   R a r e   T o n e s

The normal tones for MIDDLE consonants with live syllables are the first three, i.e. those above the row of asterisks. The last two tones are relatively rare and are found mostly in the following types of words: (1) particles, (2) onomatopoetic or affective words, (3) recent loanwords taken from Chinese or English.

B. Dead Syllables

When used with a MIDDLE consonant initiating a **dead** syllable, the same rules apply except that absence of a marker indicates the **low** tone.

MIDDLE CONSONANT WITH DEAD SYLLABLE

Marker	Value	Example	Transcription
(none)	Low	จะ	/càʔ/ will, shall
		จัด	/càd/ to prepare
		บอก	/bɔ̀ɔg/ to say to
		* * * * * * * *	
่ ̆	Falling	จะ̆	/câʔ/ yes (intimate)
		ทุบ	/tûb/ (imitative similar to Eng. "thud")
		อ้วก	/ʔûag/ (imit. of vomiting sound)
่ ́	High	โต๊ะ	/tóʔ/ table (< Chinese)
		เจ๊ก	/cég/ Chinese person (informal)(< Chin.)
		จ๊วก	/cúag/ pure (of white) (restr. modifier)
		* * * * * * * *	
		* * * * * * *	
่ ̇	Rising	จะ̇	/cǎʔ/ yes? (ans. when called--intimate)

Points to Remember

(1) The <u>first</u> tonal marker is NEVER used with dead syllables since the low tone is shown by absence of a marker.

(2) The <u>middle</u> tone does not occur with dead syllables except as an alternate pronunciation of the short-vowel subvariety known as "neutralized" syllables (p. 26).

Normal and Rare Tones

The most common tonal indication for dead syllables initiated by a MIDDLE consonant is the <u>low</u> tone shown by absence of a marker. The remaining tones occur only with particles, onomatopoetic or affective words, and with recent Chinese or English loanwords (cf. p. 28).

For all practical purposes one can say that the fourth tonal marker is NEVER used in dead syllables. The one and only such example that has been found in the recent Thai-Thai Dictionary is the one given. It is obviously a shortened or "clipped" form of /cǎa/ (see p. 28) which has the same usage.

4. Tonal Markers and HIGH Consonants

A. Live Syllables

There are only three tones used with live syllables initiated by HIGH consonants. These are the <u>rising</u> tone, shown by absence of a marker, and the <u>low</u> and <u>falling</u> tones, shown by the 1st and 2nd tonal markers, respectively. Other tones are taken care of in the writing system by the use of LOW consonants, as shown in the next section (pp. 32-34).

HIGH CONSONANT WITH LIVE SYLLABLE

Marker	Value	Example	Transcription
(none)	Rising	เขา	/khǎw/ he, she, they
่ —	Low	เข่า	/khàw/ knee
๋ —	Falling	เข้า	/khâw/ to enter

~~~~~~

B. Dead Syllables

When a HIGH consonant initiates a dead syllable absence of a tonal marker indicates the <u>low</u> tone. Any other tonal indication is RARE under these circumstances, but see the fourth example below.

HIGH CONSONANT WITH DEAD SYLLABLE

Marker	Value	Example	Transcription
(none)	Low	แฉะ	/chè?/ to be damp, wet
		สิบ	/sìb/ ten
		ถูก	/thùug/ to be right
* * * * * * * *			
๋ —	Falling	มักขัก	/mâgkhâg/ very (of degree of obesity) (restr. modifier)

~~~~~~

5. Tonal Markers and LOW Consonants

A. Live Syllables

When a LOW consonant initiates a live syllable, absence of a marker indicates the <u>middle</u> tone, the 1st marker indicates the <u>falling</u> tone, and the 2nd marker indicates the <u>high</u> tone.

<u>LOW CONSONANT WITH LIVE SYLLABLE</u>

Marker	Value	Example	Transcription
(none)	Middle	ทา	/thaa/ to smear
่ —	Falling	่ ทา	/thâa/ port
๊ —	High	๊ ทา	/tháa/ to dare

∿∿

B. Dead Syllables

When a LOW consonant initiates a dead syllable, it makes a difference whether the vowel is SHORT or LONG.

If the vowel is SHORT, absence of a marker indicates the <u>high</u> tone, and in rare instances the 1st marker is used to indicate the <u>falling</u> tone. Moreover, with vowels not normally marked as short (except in those cases where ⌃ /májtàjkhúu/ can be used; see p. 18) the 1st marker indicates a SHORT vowel under the <u>falling</u> tone.

If the vowel is LONG, absence of a marker indicates the <u>falling</u> tone, and in rare instances the 2nd marker is used to indicate the <u>high</u> tone.

LOW CONSONANT WITH SHORT VOWEL IN DEAD SYLLABLE

Marker	Value	Example	Transcription
(none)	High	ละ	/láʔ/ to abandon
		ลับ	/láb/ to be secret
	* * * * * * * *		
ั	Falling	ค่ะ	/khâʔ/ yes (woman sp.)
		มักฃัก	/mâgkhâg/ very (of degree of obesity)
		ลอกแลก	/lɔ̂glêg/ to be restless, shifty, inattentive

LOW CONSONANT WITH LONG VOWEL IN DEAD SYLLABLE

Marker	Value	Example	Transcription
(none)	Falling	พูด	/phûud/ to talk, say
	* * * * * * * *		
ั	High	เชิ้ต	/chə́əd/ shirt (< Eng.)

Rare Tones

The use of the 1st marker with a short vowel in dead syllables occurs almost exclusively with particles, and these are few in number. In any other circumstances it is extremely rare.

The use of the 2nd marker with a long vowel in dead syllables is also very rare and occurs almost exclusively in certain loanwords from English. Such

words are also sometimes spelled with the 3rd marker
instead of the 2nd, but this is considered incorrect
by many, viz.

เชิ้ท   /chə́əd/ shirt (< Eng.)

The 2nd marker is used because it is associated with
the high tone when used with LOW consonants, while
the 3rd marker is used by some because it is unam-
biguously associated with the high tone through its
use in that function with MIDDLE consonants (p. 29).

6. The Pairing of HIGH and LOW Consonants

The HIGH consonants (p. 12) are always voiceless
aspirated stops or voiceless spirants, and for each
HIGH consonant (or set of HIGH consonants identically pronounced) there is a corresponding LOW consonant
(or set of LOW consonants identically pronounced.)
This "pairing" of the HIGH and LOW aspirated stops
and spirants is shown in the chart below. The obsolete letters of the velar series are omitted.

ASPIRATED STOPS AND SPIRANTS

HIGH	ข	ฉ	ถ	ผ	ฝ	ศ ษ ส	ห
LOW	ค ฆ	ช ฌ	ท ธ	พ ภ	ฟ	ซ	ฮ

In order to learn the proper spelling of Thai
syllables beginning in aspirated stops or spirants
it is necessary to keep these two series in mind at
all times and to be able to shift from a HIGH to a
LOW aspirated stop or spirant at a moment's notice.
The reason for this is that it is impossible to in-
cate the five tones used with live syllables and

the three normally used with dead syllables without
using both series of consonants. The manner in which
this shifting takes place in live syllables is illustrated in the chart below. A DASH indicates that
the syllable having the tone indicated cannot be
written with the consonant series indicated.

LOW AND HIGH SERIES IN LIVE SYLLABLES

T ne	LOW	HIGH	Transcription
Mic ile	กาง	——	/khaaŋ/ jaw
Low	——	ข่าง	/khàaŋ/ top (toy)
Falling	ก่าง	ข๋าง	LOW /khâaŋ/ long-tailed monkey
			HIGH /khâaŋ/ side
High	ก๋าง	——	/kháaŋ/ to remain over
Rising	——	ขาง	/khǎaŋ/ egg (< Camb.)

The chart reveals that in live syllables the
falling tone may be written either way, but no other
ambiguity exists. As far as pronunciation is concerned it makes no difference whether a HIGH or a
LOW consonant is used. However, certain words must
be spelled one way, others the other way. It thus
turns out that some homonyms are distinguished in
writing by this means. But homonyms are also distinguished by employing different identically pronounced HIGH or LOW consonants.

The manner of shifting from the LOW to the HIGH
series in dead syllables is illustrated below. The
rare tones are omitted (see pp. 31 and 33).

LOW AND HIGH SERIES IN DEAD SYLLABLES

Tone	LOW	HIGH	Transcription

Short Vowel

Low	—	ขับ	/khàb/ to drive
High	ค้ับ	—	/kháb/ to be tight

Long Vowel

Low	—	แถบ	/thὲɛb/ region, section
Falling	เทบ	—	/thêɛb/ almost, nearly

7. The Conversion of Sonorants

All consonant symbols read as voiced sonorants
are inherently LOW. In order to have a means by
which all five tones may be written with syllables
beginning in a voiced sonorant it is necessary to
have some method of converting the LOW series of
voiced sonorants into HIGH consonants. The device
used for this purpose is to place the HIGH consonant ห /hɔ̌ɔ hìib/ in front of the LOW sonorant which
is to be converted. See the chart on p. 38.

When ห serves in this function it is known as
ห นำ /hɔ̌ɔ nam/ "h-preceding" (or "h-leading") and
is not pronounced. The resulting cluster of conson-

ants is then treated as a HIGH consonant and the
value of the tonal markers used is the same as for
the inherently HIGH consonants (pp. 30-31). This
is illustrated in the charts below and on the following page. The tonal markers and superscript
vowels are placed over the second consonant of the
cluster.

CONVERTED HIGH SONORANT IN LIVE SYLLABLE

Marker	Value	Example	Transcription
(none)	Rising	หนา	/năa/ to be thick
ˋ —	Low	น้อยหน่า	/nɔ́ɔjnàa/ custard apple
ˇ —	Falling	หน้า	/nâa/ face; front

~~~~~~

CONVERTED HIGH SONORANT IN DEAD SYLLABLE

Marker	Value	Example	Transcription
(none)	Low	เหมาะ	/mɔ́ʔ/ to be suitable, fit, fitting
		หยิบ	/jìb/ to pick up
		หลีก	/lìig/ to evade

~~~~~~

Just as LOW aspirated stops and spirants are
paired with HIGH aspirated stops and spirants (see
p. 34), so unconverted LOW sonorants are paired with
converted HIGH sonorants, as shown on the following

page. As far as the writer has been able to ascertain, two of the sonorants, ฌ and ฑ, do not happen to occur in converted form and they are therefore omitted.

<u>SONORANTS</u>

LOW	ง	ญ	น	ม	ย	ล	ว
HIGH	หง	หญ	หน	หม	หย	หล	หว

The chart immediately below illustrates the way in which all five of the tones may be written with syllables beginning in a voiced sonorant. Both unconverted and converted sonorants must be used, and the proper spelling of words involving the ambiguity in respect to the falling tone (compare p. 35) must always be memorized.

<u>LOW AND HIGH SONORANTS IN LIVE SYLLABLES</u>

Tone	LOW	HIGH	Transcription
Middle	นา	—	/naa/ paddy field
Low	—	น้อยหน่า	/nɔ́ɔjnàa/ custard apple
Falling	น่า	หน้า	LOW /nâa/ inducing to, -able (e.g. lov<u>able</u>)
			HIGH /nâa/ face; front
High	น้า	—	/náa/ younger maternal uncle or aunt
Rising	—	หนา	/nǎa/ to be thick

LOW AND HIGH SONORANTS IN DEAD SYLLABLES

Tone	LOW	HIGH	Transcription
Short Vowel			
Low	——	หลับ	/làb/ to close (the eyes)
High	สับ	——	/láb/ to be secret
Long Vowel			
Low	——	หมาก	/màag/ areca nut
Falling	มาก	——	/mâag/ to be much; very

〰〰〰〰〰〰〰〰〰〰〰〰〰〰〰〰〰〰〰〰〰〰〰〰〰〰〰〰〰〰〰〰〰〰〰〰

R a r e   T o n e s

Rare tones (i.e. the 1st tonal marker with a short vowel in a dead syllable and the 2nd tonal marker with a long vowel in a dead syllable) occasionally occur with unconverted LOW sonorants. The remarks on p. 33 therefore pertain to sonorants as well as to aspirated stops and spirants. Examples:

แนะ	/nê?/ (particle used to call attention to smthg.)
โน๊ต	/nóod/ notes (< Eng.)

__Comment.__ The consonant ห is not the only silent letter used for purposes of conversion. The consonant อ has a similar use in rare instances. See the following section.

8. Special Method of Converting the
Palatal Semivowel

In the modern Thai language there are <u>four</u> common words in which the sonorant ย is converted into a MIDDLE consonant by means of a preceding อ. When used in this function อ is known as อ นำ /ʔɔɔ nam/ "glottal stop-preceding" ("glottal stop-leading") and is <u>not</u> pronounced.

FOUR WORDS SPELLED WITH อ นำ

Spelling	Transcription
อย่า	/jàa/ don't, do not ... (prohibitive)
อยู่	/jùu/ to stay, remain, be at (a place)
อย่าง	/jàaŋ/ kind, sort, variety; like
อยาก	/jàag/ to wish, wish to ...

All other instances in which อ precedes a sonorant, including other instances in which it precedes ย, are covered by a different set of rules. See the discussion and examples on pp. 50 and 52-53.

<u>Comment</u>. The spelling of the four words shown above must be memorized. Two of them are homonyms with other words spelled with ห นำ, viz.

Spelling	Transcription
หย่า	/jàa/ to divorce ... (spouse)
หยาก	/jàag/ (see the two examples below)
หยากเยื่อ	/jàagjɯ̂a/ discarded material
หยากไย่	/jàagjâj/ cobwebs

CHAPTER IV

I N I T I A L   C O N S O N A N T S

1. Regular and Irregular Initial Consonants

A study of the list of consonants (pp. 6-9) shows that a great many of them have identical pronunciations in initial position. The distinction between those of the HIGH and those of the LOW series is a necessary one for the purpose of indicating the various tones (pp.34-36). But even after allowance for this distinction has been made, there still remain many consonants of identical pronunciation within the same series. It is therefore advantageous to know which of two or more identically pronounced consonants of the same series may be considered the regular spelling for a given consonant sound and which may be considered irregular. See the chart below.

Pronunciation Initially		Regular Spelling	Irregular Spelling
		S T O P S	
k-	MIDDLE	ก	——
kh-	HIGH	ข	——
kh-	LOW	ค	ฅ
c-	MIDDLE	จ	——
ch-	HIGH	ฉ	——
ch-	LOW	ช	ฌ
d-	MIDDLE	ด	ฎ. Very rarely ฑ.
t-	MIDDLE	ต	ฏ

41

Pronunciation Initially		Regular Spelling	Irregular Spelling

S T O P S (CONT.)

th-	HIGH	ฐ	ฉ
th-	LOW	ฑ	ธ, ฒ, ฐ. But ฑ is also read /d-/ MIDDLE in a few words.
b-	MIDDLE	บ	——
p-	MIDDLE	ป	——
ph-	HIGH	ผ	——
ph-	LOW	พ	ภ
?-	MIDDLE	อ	——

S P I R A N T S

s-	HIGH	ส	ศ, ษ
s-	LOW	ซ	——
f-	HIGH	ฝ	——
f-	LOW	ฟ	——
h-	HIGH	ห	——
h-	LOW	ฮ	——

S O N O R A N T S

ŋ-	LOW	ง	——
n-	LOW	น	ณ
m-	LOW	ม	——
j-	LOW	ย	ญ
r-	LOW	ร	——
l-	LOW	ล	ฬ
w-	LOW	ว	——

Most words having irregular spelling as to initial consonants are of foreign origin (particularly of Pali or Sanskrit origin), but not all such words belong in this category.

Examples of common or reasonably common words which have <u>irregular</u> spelling as to syllable-initial consonant are given below.

	Example	Transcription
ฆ–	ฆ่า	/khâa/ to kill
ฉ–	กะเฌอ	/kàchəə/ tree (< Camb.)
		Not a common word. VERY RARE cons.
ฎ–	กรกฎาคม	/kàrágkàdaakhom/ July
		Additional irregularities in this and the following examples are discussed in later sections.
ฏ–	ปฏิบัติ	/pàtìbàd/ to do, act
ฐ–	ฐานะ	/thăaná²/ status, position
ธ–	เธอ	/thəə/ you (sp. to intimates)
ท–	นาที	/naathii/ minute (of time)
		Here ท is /th-/ LOW.
	บัณฑิตย์	/bandìd/ pundit
		Here ท is /d-/ MIDDLE.
ฒ–	เฒ่า	/thâw/ to be old, aged
ภ–	ภาค	/phâag/ part, section
ษ–	ภาษา	/phaasăa/ language
ศ–	โศก	/sòog/ sorrow; to be sorrowful
ณ–	ณ	/ná²/ at, in, of (place or time)
ญ–	หญ้า	/jâa/ grass
ฬ–	กีฬา, กิฬา	/kiilaa, kìlaa/ sport(s),athletics

2. Initial Consonant Clusters
and Groupings

All sorts of consonants may be written adjacent
to one another at the beginning of the syllable but
not all of these are pronounced as consonant clusters. Therefore only those which can be pronounced
as true clusters will hereafter be called "consonant
clusters." Those which cannot be so pronounced are
termed "consonant groupings."

Syllable initial consonant clusters and groupings
fall into three general subclasses: (1) Those pronounced as true consonant clusters, p. 46; (2) those
pronounced as single consonants, pp. 47-48; and, as
the most numerous subclass, (3) those pronounced
in two syllables with intervening unwritten vowel,
pp. 49-53. There is one general tonal rule which normally holds for all of these subclasses, viz.

> If the <u>second</u> consonant is a sonorant the ini-
> tial consonant is normally the <u>governing</u> con-
> sonant and the cluster or group is classified
> as MIDDLE, HIGH, or LOW depending on the clas-
> sification of the <u>first</u> consonant. Examples:
>
> กล้า   /klâa/ to dare
>
> ขวาน   /khwǎan/ ax
>
> พร้อม   /phrɔ́ɔm/ to be ready, set

Sporadic exceptions are discussed on pp. 52-53.

The arrangement of accompanying tonal and vocalic
symbols with respect to clusters and groupings is
also important. The rules follow: (1) All vowel symbols which follow single consonants are placed after
the <u>second</u> consonant of the cluster or the grouping.
(2) Those which precede single consonants are placed

before the first consonant <u>except</u> in circumstances
described on pp. 52-53. (3) All tonal markers and
superscript vowel symbols are written over the second consonant. (4) All subscript vowel symbols are
written under the second consonant. (5) Each part
of a complex vowel symbol is subject to that one of
the preceding rules which is appropriate to it. The
examples below illustrate these rules in order.

(1)	ปลา	/plaa/	fish
	ตลาด	/tàlàad, ta-/	market
(2)	แปล	/plɛɛ/	to translate
	เพลง	/phleeŋ/	song
(3)	ครั้ง	/khráŋ/	time, instance
	ชนิด	/cháníd, cha-/	kind, sort
(4)	ครู	/khruu/	teacher
(5)	เพราะ	/phrɔ́?/	because
	เสมอ	/sàmɤ̌ə, sa-/	to be even; always

Syllables which begin in a consonant cluster or
grouping and contain the short unwritten o-vowel
followed by a consonant will be written as three consonants in a row, e.g.

กลม	/klom/	to be round
ถนน	/thànǒn, tha-/	street

3. True Consonant Clusters

The phonetic composition of true consonant clusters is (1) an unaspirated or aspirated <u>voiceless</u>
stop followed by (2) /r/, /l/, or /w/. The chart on
the following page shows the permissible clusters

arranged according to series (as determined by the first consonant).

PERMISSIBLE CONSONANT CLUSTERS

MIDDLE	กร	กล	กว	ตร	ปร	ปล
HIGH	ขร	ขล	ขว		ผร	ผล
LOW	คร	คล	คว		พร	พล

Examples

กร–	กรง	/kroŋ/ cage
กล–	กล้า	/klâa/ to dare
กว–	กว่า	/kwàa/ more than
ตร–	ตรง	/troŋ/ to be straight
ปร–	ประตู	/pràtuu, pra-/ door
ปล–	ปลา	/plaa/ fish
ขร–	เจ้าขรัว	/câwkhrŭa/ rich man
ขล–	โขลง	/khlŏoŋ/ herd (of elephants)
ขว–	ขวา	/khwăa/ right (side)
ผร–		RARE
ผล–	แผล	/phlɛ̌ɛ/ (a) wound
คร–	เครื่อง	/khrŷaŋ/ instrumentation
คล–	คล้าย	/khláaj/ to resemble
คว–	ควัน	/khwan/ smoke
พร–	พรุ่งนี้	/phrûŋníi/ tomorrow
พล–	พลอย	/phlɔɔj/ precious stone

Note that some of the "irregular" initial consonants (pp. 41-42) coinciding in pronunciation with some

of those above (e.g. ฎ, ฐ, ฏ, ฑ, ฒ) do not happen
to occur in true clusters.

4. Special Initial Consonant Groupings
Pronounced as Single Consonants

Initial consonant groupings pronounced as single
consonants always have ร as their <u>second</u> consonant.
In general one need only remember that the ร is silent. One combination, however, is unique in that
the pronounced consonant bears no relation to either
of the component written consonants (rule 1 below).

Rule 1. The combination ทร- is usually pronounced
/s/ and the series is LOW.

Pronounced /s-/ LOW

ทร—	ทราย	/saaj/ (1) sand. (2) hog-deer
	ทราบ	/sâab/ to know (elegant word)
	ไทร	/saj/ banyan (tree)
	ทรง	/soŋ/ (1) form, structure. (2) Pre-cedes verbs if sp. of royalty.
	ทรัพย์	/sáb/ wealth, money
		(The new symbol ´ is a cancellation sign, p. 63.)
	ทรุด	/sûd/ to subside, drop (as into chair)
	กระทรวง	/kràsuaŋ, kra-/ ministry (of gov't)

Rule 2. The combinations ศร— and สร— are usually
pronounced /s/, HIGH series.

Pronounced /s-/ HIGH

ศร—	ศรี	/sǐi/ splendor, excellence, glory
	เศรษฐกิจ	/sèedthàkìd, -tha-/ economics

ศร— เศรษฐี   /sèedthĭi/ rich person, millionaire

เศร้า   /sâw/ to be sad, sorrowful

โศกเศร้า   /sòogsâw/ to be sad, sorrowful

สร— สร้อย   /sɔ̂ɔj/ neck ornament, bracelet

สร่าง   /sàaŋ/ to get sober

สร้าง   /sâaŋ/ to build, construct

เสร็จ   /sèd/ to be finished, through

ประเสริฐ   /pràsə̀əd, pra-/ to be excellent

สระ   /sà?/ (1) pond. (2) to shampoo

<u>Comment</u>. The last example above, comprising
two homonyms, is additionally a homograph with
still another word of different pronunciation
and meaning (see the rules on pp. 49-50), viz.

สระ   /sàrà?, sa-/ vowel

Rule 3. In one important and very common word the
combination จร— is pronounced /c/, MIDDLE series.

Pronounced /c-/ MIDDLE

จร— จริง   /ciŋ/ to be true, sincere

In other instances this combination is not so pronounced (see p. 50).

E x c e p t i o n s

Every one of the combinations discussed in this
section can also be pronounced in accordance with
the rules given in the immediately following section (pp. 49-50). The spelling rules are therefore
entirely <u>arbitrary</u> and the examples in both sections
must be memorized for ease in reading and writing.

5. Initial Consonant Groupings Pronounced in Two Syllables

Initial consonant groupings which <u>are</u> not or cannot be pronounced as true clusters (pp. 45-46) or as single consonants (pp. 47-48) are pronounced in two syllables by the intrusion of an unwritten vowel after the first of the two consonants. In most cases this intruded vowel is /-a-/, as described below; but in rare instances it is /-ɔɔ-/ ~ /-ɔ-/, as discussed on pp. 51-52.

The normal rules for determining the tones of the intruded syllable and the syllable which follows it are given below with examples. Exceptions are illustrated on pp. 52-53.

A. HIGH Consonant Preceding

A preceding HIGH consonant converts a following low sonorant into a HIGH consonant. Both syllables are then pronounced according to the rules for HIGH consonants. In rapid speech, however, the first syllable (containing the intruded /-a-/) is subject to a neutralization of tone. This means that the vowel is pronounced on a middle tone. This pronunciation is shown below as a variant after a comma.

เสมอ	/sǎmɤ̌ə, sa-/ to be even; always
เสมียน	/sǎmǐan, sa-/ clerk, office worker
ถนน	/thǎnǒn, tha-/ street, road
ฝรั่ง	/fàràŋ, fa-/ Occidental
ขยี้	/khàjîi, kha-/ to squeeze, crush
สนุก	/sànùg, sa-/ to have fun, be amused
แผนก	/phànɛ̀ɛg, pha-/ department
ฉลาด	/chàlàad, cha-/ to be clever

B. MIDDLE Consonant Preceding

A preceding MIDDLE consonant converts a following LOW sonorant into a MIDDLE consonant. Both syllables are then pronounced according to the rules for MIDDLE consonants. In rapid speech the first syllable is subject to neutralization.

เจริญ	/càrəən, ca-/ to progress, advance
ตลิ่ง	/tàlìŋ, ta-/ bank, shore
อร่อย	/ʔàrɔ̀j, ʔa-/ to be delicious
องุ่น	/ʔàŋùn, ʔa-/ grape
กนก	/kànòg, ka-/ gold (literary word)
ตลก	/tàlòg, ta-/ to be amusing, humorous
ตลาด	/tàlàad, ta-/ market, market place
จมูก	/càmùug, ca-/ nose

C. Unconverted Consonants

With all other combinations of consonants no conversions take place. Therefore each of the two consonants governs the tone of its own syllable in accordance with the rules for its own series, whatever that may be. In rapid speech neutralization occurs.

สบาย	/sàbaaj, sa-/ to be well, comfortable
สติ	/sàtìʔ, sa-/ mind, consciousness
สถานี	/sàthǎanii, sa-/ station (railroad)
สหาย	/sàhǎaj, sa-/ friend
สภา	/sàphaa, sa-/ house, body (organization)
เฉพาะ	/chàphɔ́ʔ, cha-/ to be special
ทหาร	/tháhǎan, tha-/ soldier, member of an armed force

ชนิด /cháníd, cha-/ kind, sort, variety

หม่า /phámâa, pha-/ Burma; Burmese

นรก /nárók, na-/ hell

D. Variations in Spelling

Prior to the appearance of the latest Thai dictionary issued by the Ministry of Education in 1950,
some of the words listed under C above were spelled
with written —ะ inserted after the first consonant.
The McFarland Thai-English Dictionary, widely used
by English-speaking students of Thai, was issued before the time of this change and therefore has the
old spelling for such words. A few examples are:

New Way Old Way Transcription

เฉพาะ ฉะเพาะ /chàphɔ́ʔ, cha-/ to be special

ชนิด ชะนิด /cháníd, cha-/ kind, sort, variety

หม่า พะม่า /phámâa, pha-/ Burma; Burmese

Many other words having similar sound combinations
are still spelled with —ะ, e.g.

ชะนี /chánii, cha-/ gibbon

ทะเล /thálee, tha-/ sea

For other examples the student is referred to the
writer's THAI VOCABULARY (ACLS, 1955).

6. The Intruded Vowel /-ɔɔ-/ ~ /-ɔ-/

In special cases an initial consonant grouping
which cannot be pronounced as a true consonant cluster is pronounced in two syllables by the intrusion
of /-ɔɔ-/ or sometimes /-ɔ-/ in rapid speech if the
first consonant is MIDDLE or LOW. Most of the group-

ings which come in this category contain บ, ม, ท,
or ธ followed by ร, but other types of examples occur sporadically. (Any additional spelling irregularities in the examples below are taken up later.)

บ–	บรม	/bɔɔrom, bɔ-/ supreme
	บริบูรณ์	/bɔɔríbuun, bɔ-/ to be complete
	บริเวณ	/bɔɔríween, bɔ-/ environs, vicinity
	บริษัท	/bɔɔrísàd, bɔ-/ company, firm
	บริสุทธิ์	/bɔɔrísùd, bɔ-/ to be pure
	อธิบดี	/ʔàthíbɔɔdii, ʔa-..-bɔ-/ head of a department
ม–	มรกต	/mɔɔrákòd, mɔra-/ emerald
	มรดก	/mɔɔrádòg, mɔra-/ inheritance
	มรสุม	/mɔɔrásǔm, mɔra-/ monsoon
ท–	ทรมาน	/thɔɔrámaan, thɔra-/ to persecute
ธ–	ธรณี	/thɔɔránii, thɔra-/ the world, earth
จ–	จระเข้	/cɔɔrákhêe, cɔra-/ crocodile
ม–	มหรสพ	/máhɔɔrásòb, ma-..-ra-/ (an) enter-tainment

7. Exceptions in the Treatment of Consonant Groupings

It may be stated as a general rule that an initial HIGH or MIDDLE consonant will govern the tone
of a following LOW sonorant when no **written** vowel
intervenes (pp. 49-50), but this rule is **not** an in-
variable one. In some cases a following LOW sonorant will remain LOW. In such cases, too, the normally preposed เ– and โ– vowels will be placed in
front of the **second** instead of the first consonant;

see, for instance, the third example cited below.

The unconverted LOW sonorant is underlined in the phonetic transcription below. Any additional spelling irregularities are explained later.

Unconverted LOW Sonorants

สมาคม	/sàmaakhom, sa-/	club, society
สมาชิก	/sàmaachíg, sa-/	member (of a club)
สโมสร	/sàmoosɔ̌ɔn, sa-/	club, association
พาหนะ	/phaahàná?, -ha-/	vehicle
ไปรษณีย์	/prajsànii, -sa-/	mail, post
อนุยาต	/ʔànújâad, ʔa-/	to permit, allow
อนุมัติ	/ʔànúmád, ʔa-/	permission
อยุธยา	/ʔàjúdthájaa, ʔa-..-tha-/	Ayutthaya (Ayuthia)

It may also be stated as a general rule that when two consonants which are written together comprise a permissible consonant cluster they will be pronounced as such (p. 46). But here again there are exceptions, as shown in the examples below.

Consonant Groupings Instead of Clusters

กรุณา	/kàrúnaa, ka-/	mercifulness
กวี	/kàwii, ka-/	poet
ปริมาณ	/pàrímaan, pa-/	quantity, supply
ปริญญา	/pàrinjaa, pa-/	diploma, degree
อันตราย	/ʔantàraaj, -ta-/	harm, injury
พละ	/phálá?, pha-/	(physical) strength

Many other examples of such exceptions can be found in any dictionary, but most words of this type are literary or otherwise specialized.

CHAPTER V

F I N A L   A N D   M E D I A L   C O N S O N A N T S

1. Voiced Sonorants in Final Position

There are ten voiced sonorant symbols whose pronunciation in initial position is the same as the
initial letter of the name attached to the symbol.
As far as spelling is concerned all of these may
occur in syllable final as well as syllable initial
position. However, the only sonorant sounds which
can normally occur in final position are /-j, -w,
-ŋ, -n, -m/. Because of this limitation some of
the written symbols have a special pronunciation
when occurring in syllable final position, as shown
in the chart below.

VOICED SONORANTS IN FINAL POSITION

Symbol	ง	ญ ณ น ฑ ฒ ร	ม	ย	ว
Phon. Value when Final	-ŋ	-n	-m	-j	-w

The regular spelling for final /-n/ is น as is shown
by underlining in the chart above. The other symbols
represent irregular spelling. The symbol ญ was ori-
ginally a palatal nasal /ñ/, but it is now pronounced
as a palatal semivowel /j-/ in initial position and
as a dental nasal /-n/ in final position. The symbols ฑ, ฒ, and ร are all pronounced /-n/, their hom-
organic nasal, when found in syllable final position.

Examples of important words having irregular
spelling in respect to syllable final voiced sonorants are shown on the following page.

54

Irregular Final Sonorants

—ณ	ประมาณ	/pràmaan/	about, approximately
	คุณ	/khun/	you (to equals); (title placed before given name); goodness
—ญ	สำคัญ	/sǎmkhan/	to be important
	สัญญา	/sǎnjaa/	to promise
—ล	ตาล	/taan/	sugar palm (tree)
	รัฐบาล	/rádthàbaan, -tha-/	the government (see p. 61 also)
—ฬ	ปลาวาฬ	/plaawaan/	whale
—ร	การ	/kaan/	work; act of ...-ing
	ทหาร	/tháhǎan, tha-/	soldier
	อาหาร	/ʔaahǎan/	food
	ควร	/khuan/	ought to, should

Exceptions. Some speakers of Thai who have learned English will sometimes pronounce final /-l/ in English loanwords. For such words two pronunciations are shown, e.g.

ฟุตบอลล	/fúdbɔɔn ~ fúdbɔɔl/	football (< Eng.)

2. Special Rules Concerning —ร and —รร

When a single ร follows another consonant and at the same time stands at the end of the syllable it is pronounced /-ɔɔn/. Important examples are:

พร	/phɔɔn/	blessing, blessings
อักษร	/ʔàgsɔ̌ɔn/	letter of the alphabet
นคร	/nákhɔɔn, na-/	city
ละคร	/lákhɔɔn, la-/	play, drama
สโมสร	/sàmoosɔ̌ɔn, sa-/	club, association
ถาวร	/thǎawɔɔn/	to be permanent, enduring

When double ร follows a consonant it is pronounced (1) as /-an/ if no other pronounced consonant follows in the <u>same</u> syllable, and (2) as /-a-/
if another pronounced consonant does follow. Double
ร is often referred to as ร หัน /rɔɔ hăn/. Examples:

Double ร read as /-an/

กรรไกร   /kankraj/ scissors

บรรจุ   /bancù?/ to fill

บรรทุก   /banthúg/ to load, load onto

บรรเทา   /banthaw/ to get relief, be relieved

สวรรค์   /sàwăn, sa-/ heaven

Double ร read as /-a-/

กรรม   /kam/ misfortune; object (of a verb)

กสิกรรม   /kàsìkam, ka-/ agriculture

ธรรม   /tham/ Buddhist teaching, dharma

ธรรมดา   /thammádaa, -ma-/ to be common, ordinary (see p. 60)

3. Stops and Spirants in Final Position

There are thirty-four consonant symbols for stops
and spirants. Of these, two of the velar stops are
no longer used in any position (p. 6) and an additional six are never written in final position as consonants to be pronounced. In other words, they do not
function as syllable-closing consonants. These six
consonants are the following:

ฌ   ฑ   ฒ   ห   อ   ฮ

Although อ does not occur in final position as a
consonant symbol, it does occur at the end of sylla-

bles as part or all of certain <u>vowel</u> symbols (p. 21).

The remaining twenty-six symbols for stops and spirants occur as <u>written</u> symbols in final position, but the majority of them have a different pronunciation in this position from what they have in syllable initial position. The reason for this is that in normal Thai speech voiceless aspirated and unaspirated stops and voiceless spirants do not occur as pronounced consonants in final position. The only stops which can be pronounced in this position are the voiced stops /-b, -d, -g/ and the glottal stop /-ʔ/. Final /-ʔ/ is not indicated by a definite consonant symbol in the writing system, but is represented instead by the —ะ symbol employed for short vowels not followed by a syllable-closing consonant (pp. 15 and 17). There is therefore nothing further to be explained about this sound as far as the writing system is concerned. The rules for the remaining stops and spirants occurring in final position are as follows:

(1) Words which have <u>regular</u> spelling for the stop sounds in final position employ ก for /-g/, ด for /-d/, and บ for /-b/.

(2) All other types of <u>written</u> final stops and spirants are pronounced as /-g, -d, -b/ depending upon their position of articulation. Hence all having the velar position are pronounced /-g/, all in the palatal and dental (including retroflex) position are pronounced /-d/, and all having the labial position are pronounced /-b/. See the summary chart which is presented on the following page.

58

STOPS AND SPIRANTS IN FINAL POSITION

	Velar	Palatal	Dental Retro.	Dent.	Labial
Voiced Stops			ฎ	ด	บ
Voiceless Unaspirated Stops	ก	จ	ฏ	ต	ป
Voiceless Aspirated Stops	ข ฆ ฅ ฃ	ช ฌ	ฑ ฒ ฎ ฐ	ถ ฑ ท ธ	พ ภ ฝ
Voiceless Spirants		ศ ษ ส ซ			ฟ
PHONETIC VALUE	-g	-d			-b

The six symbols mentioned on p. 56 as not occurring
in final position are omitted from the chart. The
symbols employed in regular spelling are enlarged.
Examples of words having irregular spelling with respect to final stops and spirants are shown below.

Irregular Final Stops and Spirants

—ข	เลข	/lêeg/ numeral, figure
—ค	โรค	/rôog/ disease
—ฆ	เมฆ	/mêeg/ cloud
—จ	ตรวจ	/trùad/ to inspect, examine
—ช	พืช	/phŷyd/ vegetation, plants
—ฎ	กฎ	/kòd/ rule, law
—ฏ	ปรากฏ	/praakòd/ to appear, become manifest
—ฐ	รัฐ	/rád/ state, nation

—ฆ	ฆุฆ	/wúd/	to grow, prosper (literary)
—ก	ชีวิต	/chiiwíd/	life
—ด	รถ	/ród/	car
—ท	บาท	/bàad/	baht, tical (monetary unit)
—ธ	โกรธ	/kròod/	to be angry
—ป	รูป	/rûub/	picture; form, shape
—พ	ภาพ	/phâab/	picture, image
—ภ	ลาภ	/lâab/	acquisition, gain, fortune
—ศ	ประเทศ	/pràthêed, pra-/	country (nation)
—ษ	โทษ	/thôod/	punishment
—ส	รส	/ród/	taste, flavor

Exceptions

Some speakers of Thai who have learned English sometimes pronounce syllable final /-f/ and /-s/ in recent English loanwords. For such words two pronunciations are shown, e.g.

กอล์ฟ   /kɔ́ɔb ~ kɔ́ɔf/ golf (< Eng.)

เทนนิส   /thenníd ~ thennís/ tennis (< Eng.)

4. Medial Consonants Having Double Function

Some medial consonants which stand before another consonant, as far as spelling is concerned, have a double function which may be described as follows:

(1) The consonant is pronounced at the end of the syllable in conformance with the rules given for finals on pp. 54-55 (sonorants) and pp. 56-59 (stops and spirants), and

(2) the consonant is pronounced a second time as
a syllable on its own account with the addition
of an intruded /-a-/ after the manner of initial
consonant groupings pronounced in two syllables
(see paragraphs A and B below); or, in rarer instances, it initiates a new syllable pronounced
with following written vowel (paragraph C below).

Because of the limitations on the phonetic level in
respect to permitted final consonants, a medial consonant with double function often has two different
sounds, one in its function as a syllable final consonant and another in its function as a syllable initial consonant. The rules for the tones on the intruded syllable (if any) and on the syllable which
follows it are the same as those for initial consonant groupings pronounced in two syllables (pp. 49-50).

A. Medial Sonorants with Double Function

-ณ- คุณภาพ /khunnáphâab, -na-/ quality

วัณโรค /wannárôog, -na-/ tuberculosis

-น- ทินกร /thinnákɔɔn, -na-/ the sun (elegant)

-ม- คมนาคม /khommánaakhom, -ma-/ communication

กรรมการ /kammákaan, -ma-/ committee

ธรรมดา /thammádaa, -ma-/ to be common, ordinary

-ร- ภรรยา /phanrájaa, -ra-/ wife (elegant)

Here the second ร of a double ร has
double function. See Comment 2 and
also paragraph D below.

-ล- ผลไม้ /phǒnlámáaj, -la-/ fruit (elegant)

พลเมือง /phonlámyaŋ, -la-/ population

-ย- อวัยวะ /ʔàwajjáwáʔ, ʔa-...-ja-/ organ (of the
body)

Comment <u>1</u>. จ, ญ, ฬ and ว are not found in medial position with double function.

Comment <u>2</u>. ร does not occur in this function except when double ร is involved. Instead medial ร followed by another written consonant is pronounced in some words as /-n/ (i.e. as a syllable final) and in other words as /-rá-/ (i.e. as a syllable in its own right), but not in both functions, e.g.

มารกา   /maan̲daa/ mother (elegant)

สารบาญ   /sǎarábaan, -ra-/ table of contents

B. Medial Stops and Spirants with Double Function

—ก— ปรกติ   /prògkàtì?, -ka-/ to be normal

ตุกตา   /túgkàtaa, -ka-/ doll

สกปรก   /sògkàpròg, -ka-/ to be dirty

—จ— กิจการ   /kìdcàkaan, -ca-/ work, activity

—ช— ราชการ   /râadchákaan, -cha-/ gov't service

—ฐ— รัฐบาล   /rádthàbaan, -tha-/ the government

—ฒ— วัฒนา   /wádthánaa, -tha-/ to progress

—ต— จัตวา   /càdtàwaa, -ta-/ four (eleg. and tech.)

—ท— วิทยา   /wídthájaa, -tha-/ a science

—ธ— อยุธยา   /?àjúdthájaa, ?a-...-tha-/ Ayutthaya (Ayuthia)

—ป— สัปดาห์   /sàbpàdaa, -pa-/ week (elegant)

อุปสรรค   /?ùbpàsàg, -pa-/ obstacle, difficulty

—พ— ภาพยนต์   /phâabphájon, -pha-/ motion pictures (eleg.)

อพยพ   /?òbphájób, -pha-/ to emigrate

—ศ— เทศบาล   /thêedsàbaan, -ssa-/ municipality

Medial ศ, ษ or ส may be pronounced as -ssa- instead of -dsa- in rapid speech.

ปราศจาก /prâadsàcâag, -ssa-/ without

–ษ– โฆษณา /khôodsànaa, -ssa-/ to advertize

Here ษ does not govern; see p. 52 and contrast with the next example.

–ศ– ศาสนา /sàadsànaa, -ssa-/ a religion

Sometimes double function involves a medial consonant cluster, e.g.

จักรยาน /càgkràjaan, -kra-/ bicycle

C. Double Function without Intruded Vowel

In some cases double function is found without the addition of an intruded vowel, e.g.

พระเชตุพน /phráchêedtùphon/ name of a temple

ศัตรู /sàdtruu/ enemy, foe

อัตรา /ʔàdtraa/ rate (as of exchange)

มาตรา /mâadtraa/ system (as of measurement)

สถิติ /sàthìdtìʔ, sa-/ statistics

D. Suppression of Double Function

Some words which were formerly pronounced with double function are now usually pronounced without it, and a few words fluctuate in pronunciation.

ภรรยา /phanrájaa ~ phanjaa/ wife (elegant)

ราชบุรี /râadbùrii/ Ratburi (name of a town)

เพชรบุรี /phédbùrii/ Phetburi (name of a town)

Until fairly recently the last two examples were often pronounced /râadchábùrii, -cha-/ and /phédchábùrii, -cha-/, respectively.

5. Cancellation of Final Consonants

A special symbol — known by the two names given below is often used to show that a final consonant is not to be pronounced.

ไม้ทัณฑฆาต /májthanthákhâad/ cancellation sign

การันต์ /kaaran/ cancellation sign

A consonant that is so cancelled is called by its name followed by the term /kaaran/, e.g.

ต์ /tɔɔ kaaran/ in the word การันต์.

Examples of Cancelled Final Consonants

ทุกข์ /thúg/ sorrow, misery

สตางค์ /sàtaaŋ, sa-/ stang, 1-100th tical

รถยนต์ /ródjon/ automobile

ศัพท์ /sàb/ vocabulary, words

กุมภาพันธ์ /kumphaaphan/ February

พิมพ์ /phim/ to print

บริบูรณ์ /bɔɔríbuun, bɔ-/ to be complete

สัตว์ /sàd/ animal, beast

สัตย์ /sàd/ honesty

ทรัพย์ /sáb/ wealth, money

แพทย์ /phêɛd/ physician, doctor (elegant)

วันอาทิตย์ /wan?aathíd/ Sunday

วันศุกร์ /wansùg/ Friday

วันเสาร์ /wansǎw/ Saturday

สัปดาห์ /sàbpàdaa, -pa-/ week (elegant)

วงศ์ /woŋ/ race, family, stock

ปอนด์ /pɔɔn/ pound (weight, money) (< Eng.)

Sometimes two final consonants are silenced even though only the last is marked as such by the use of the cancellation sign, e.g.

วันจันทร์ /wancan/ Monday

ราษฎร์ /râad/ realm

ศาสตร์ /sàad/ branch or field of knowledge, as in the example below.

ภูมิศาสตร์ /phuumísàad/ geography

If the cancellation sign is placed over a consonant with superscript or subscript vowel, both are rendered silent. Combinations often so treated are —ิ์ and —ุ,e.g.

สิทธิ์ /sìd/ rights, privileges

Also สิทธิ /sìdthí?/

บริสุทธิ์ /bɔɔrísùd, bɔ-/ to be pure

วัดโพธิ์ /wád phoo/ Wat Pho (famous temple)

พันธุ์ /phan/ kind, breed, species

Sometimes a preceding consonant with superscript vowel is also rendered silent, e.g.

กษัตริย์ /kàsàd, ka-/ king

6. Unmarked Final Silent Consonants

The cancellation sign is <u>not</u> <u>invariably</u> used to mark a final silent consonant. Sometimes a final consonant is silent even though unmarked. Such un-marked final silent consonant is most often ร pre-ceded by a stop, e.g.

จักร /càg/ machine (usually in compounds)

สมัคร /sàmàg, sa-/ to volunteer. Also สมัค.

เพชร /phéd/ diamond. See also p. 72.

บุตร   /bùd/ son (elegant)

บัตร   /bàd/ card (as postcard)

มิตร   /míd/ friend

มหาสมุทร /máhǎasàmùd, ma-..-sa-/ ocean

An unusual type of example is seen in

ครรภ   /khan/ pregnancy, uterus (elegant)

This is the official spelling, but the spelling ครรภ์
i.e. with — added, is the one most often seen.

7. Unmarked Nonfinal Silent Consonants

Since the cancellation sign is very rarely used
over any but final silent consonants, most types of
nonfinal silent consonants are unmarked in any way.
The silent consonant is often, but not always, ร.

(ร) สามารถ   /sǎamâad/ to be able, capable

     ปรารถนา /pràadthànǎa, -tha-/ to desire, wish

     เกียรติยศ /kìadtìjód/ honor

     ศีรษะ   /sǐisà?/ head (eleg.). Also ศีรษะ.

(ห) พราหมณ์ /phraam/ Brahman

(ฌ) เพชฌฆาต /phédchákhâad, -cha-/ executioner

Exceptions

Even though it is an exceptional usage the cancellation sign is sometimes found with nonfinal consonants, e.g. in the alternate spelling of the elegant term for "head" above. In particular it is so
used in recent loanwords from English. But some such
words are spelled now with and now without the cancellation sign, e.g.

กอล์ฟ, กอลฟ /kɔ́ɔb ~ kɔ́ɔf/ golf (< Eng.)

ฟอร์ม /fɔɔm/ form (e.g. a printed form); uniform (for a servant)(< Eng.)

8. Final Consonants with Silent Vowels

Sometimes a final subscript ╤ or superscript ╤ is silent even though there is no special symbol which can be used to indicate this. The combinations most often found are ╼ฤ and ╼ดิ, but ╼ดิ, ╼ฎิ and ╼มิ are also found, e.g.

╼ฤ	เหตุ	/hèed/	reason, cause
	ธาตุ	/thâad/	element
╼ดิ	ชาติ	/châad/	nationality, race
	ญาติ	/jâad/	relative, kin
	เกียรติ	/kìad/	honor
	อนุมัติ	/ʔànúmád, ʔa-/	permission
	ประวัติ	/pràwàd/	description, history. See p. 78.
	สมมุติ	/sǒmmúd/	to suppose
╼ดิ	จักรพรรดิ	/càgkràphád, -kra-/	emperor
╼ฎิ	โกฏิ	/kòod/	ten million
╼มิ	อุณหภูมิ	/ʔunnáhàphuum, -naha-/	temperature

Sometimes the vowel remains silent when the word is compounded with another word, e.g.

เหตุการณ์	/hèedkaan/	events, circumstances
ภูมิรู้	/phuumrúu/	knowledge, education (in a person)

But at other times the vowel is pronounced, e.g.

ภูมิศาสตร์	/phuumísàad/	geography
เกียรติยศ	/kìadtìjód/	honor
ประวัติศาสตร์	/pràwàdtìsàad, pra-/	history (subject)

CHAPTER VI

O T H E R   I R R E G U L A R I T I E S

1. Special Consonant + Vowel Symbols

There are two sets of special consonant + vowel symbols which are shown below. In <u>theory</u> these symbols are treated as vowels and both short and long varieties occur. In <u>practice</u> they are treated as consonant + vowel symbols and the consonantal component behaves like a LOW consonant.

Short Symbol	Name	Long Symbol	Name
ฤ	/rýʔ/	ฤๅ	/ryy/
ฦ	/lýʔ/	ฦๅ	/lyy/

The most common of these symbols is ฤ /rýʔ/ and it may be pronounced /ry-/, /ri-/ or /rəə-/ depending upon the individual word in which it is used. It occurs as a syllable initial or as the second component of any MIDDLE or LOW consonant cluster in which ร occurs as the second component (see p. 46). It also occurs clustered with ห, a combination in which ร does not occur.

Examples of ฤ as Syllable Initial

ฤกู	/rýduu/ season
ฤทธิ์	/ríd/ supernatural power
ฤกษ์	/rəəg/ auspicious time

67

Examples of ฤ in Clusters

อังกฤษ	/ʔaŋkrìd/ England; English
ประพฤติ	/pràphrýd, pra-/ to behave, act
วันพฤหัสบดี	/wan phrýhàdsàbɔɔdii, -ssabɔ-/ Thursday (see p. 61)
พฤษภาคม	/phrýdsàphaakhom -ssa-/ May
พฤศจิกายน	/phrýdsàcikaajon, -ssa-/ November
ทฤษฎี	/thrídsàdii, -ssa-/ theory

The long symbol ฤๅ is very rarely used. It occurs in the example cited below, but the same word
is also spelled with the short symbol at times.

ฤๅษี, ฤษี   /ryysǐi/ or /rýsǐi/ hermit, anchorite

The symbols ฦ and ฦๅ are virtually never used.
There are therefore no useful, or even moderately
useful, examples which can be cited. The symbols
are often omitted entirely from Thai dictionaries.

<u>Dictionary</u> <u>Order</u>. Since these symbols are not
true consonants but consonant + vowel symbols, they
do not comprise a part of the inventory of consonants (pp. 6-9). For the purpose of order of arrangement in dictionaries, ฤ and ฤๅ succeed ร, while ฦ
and ฦๅ are placed after ล.

2. The Twenty Words Spelled with ใ-

The complete list of the twenty words which must
be spelled with the symbol ใ- is given on the following page. The arrangement follows the Thai alphabetical order. Most of these words are very common and
none of them are uncommon, so the proper spelling of
all of them must be memorized.

TWENTY WORDS SPELLED WITH ใ–

ใกล้	/klâj/	to be close, near
ใคร	/khraj/	who? someone, anyone
ใคร่	/khrâj/	desire to, wish to
ใจ	/caj/	heart, mind, spirit (fig. sense)
ใช่	/châj/	to be ...; that's so!
ใช้	/cháj ~ cháaj/	to use ...; to be used
ใด	/daj/	which, any (preceded by clf.)
ใต้	/tâj/	to be under, southern
ใน	/naj/	in (space); in, at, on (time)
ใบ	/baj/	leaf (in cpds. exc. when a clf.)
ใบ้	/bâj/	dumb, mute
ใฝ่, หมกใฝ่	/fàj/, as in /fàgfàj/	to be engrossed in
ใย	/jaj/	fiber; web (of spider)
สะใภ้	/sàpháj, sa-/	female rel. by marriage
ใส	/sǎj/	to be clear, transparent
ใส่	/sàj/	to put in, insert
ให้	/hâj/	to give ...; for ...
ใหญ่	/jàj/	to be big, large
ใหม่	/màj/	to be new; anew
ใหล, หลงใหล	/lǎj/, only in /lǒŋlǎj/	to be infatuated with ...

Some of these have homonyms spelled with ไ– as in the examples shown below:

ไจ	/caj/	skein (of thread, yarn)
ไก, บันไก	/daj/, as in /bandaj/	stairs
ไต้	/tâj/	torch

ไน /naj/ spinning wheel

ไย /jaj/ why, for what

ไส /sǎj/ to push, shove (forward, away)

ไห้, ร้องไห้ /hâj/, as in /rɔ́ɔŋhâj/ to cry, weep

ไหล /lǎj/ to flow

3. More About Unwritten /-a-/

A. Unwritten —ะ

In previous chapters examples have been given of intruded /-a-/ in initial consonant groupings (see pp. 49-51) and after certain medial consonants with double function (see pp. 60-61). Single consonants or word final consonants may also be pronounced with an unwritten /-a?/, but most such words are highly literary. One of the most commonly seen words of this type is the following:

ณ /ná?/ at, in (of time or place)

Other examples are very much rarer:

ศิลป /sǐnlápà?/ arts, crafts

ติล /tìlá?/ sesame (literary word; the common word is งา /ŋaa/)

B. Unwritten —ั/

Another rare type of unwritten /-a-/ is found in the case of a few words which are pronounced as if they were spelled with —ั/. Among words of this type which have a fairly high frequency the first two examples below are perhaps the most important.

สตรี /sàdtrii/ woman (elegant)

กรกฎาคม /kàrágkàdaakhom, ka-...-ka-/ July

อกตัญญู /?àgkàtanjuu, -ka-/ to be ungrateful

The usual reading for the unwritten vowel in a
closed syllable is /-o-/, as shown on pp. 18-20.
The reading /-a-/ shown in the three examples on
the preceding page is very rare. The pressure for
the /-o-/ reading is such that some words which
were until recently read with /-a-/ are now usually
read with /-o-/, e.g.

ึคมนาคม   /khommánaakhom, -na-/ communication

มกราคม   /mógkàraakhom, -ka-/ January

The two words were formerly (or rarely still are)
pronounced /khammánaakhom, -na-/ and /mágkàraakhom,
-ka-/, respectively.

4. The Use of the Vowel-Shortening Symbol

The vowel-shortening symbol ⌣, known as ไม้ไต่คู้
(see p. 18), has certain important restrictions as
to its use. It is used in combination with the vowels เ–, แ–, and –อ (and no others), and it is used
with these only if two additional conditions are met,
viz. (1) there must be a syllable-final consonant,
and (2) there must be no tonal marker required in
the writing of the syllable. The vowel-shortening
symbol is most commonly used with เ–, e.g.

VOWEL-SHORTENING SYMBOL WITH เ–

เก็บ   /kèb/ to pick, gather, collect ...

เจ็ด   /cèd/ seven

เช็ด   /chéd/ to wipe ...

เร็ว   /rew/ to be fast, quick, rapid

เล็ก   /lég/ to be small, little

เห็น   /hěn/ to see ...

เหล็ก   /lèg/ iron (metal)

Exceptions

One important word, /pen/ (1st example below) is
spelled with ⌐ in dictionaries, official writings,
textbooks, etc., but is normally spelled without ⌐
in newspapers. This is occasioned in large part by
the high frequency of its occurrence. The remaining
words shown below are regularly spelled without ⌐
under all circumstances.

เป็น, เปน	/pen/ to be ...
เพชร	/phéd/ diamond. (See also p. 64.)
เมตร	/méd/ meter (< French)
เมตริก	/médtríg/ metric (< French)

The use of ⌐ with the vowels แ- and -อ is much
rarer. Although there are some important exceptions,
its use with these two vowels is largely confined to
imitative words, restricted modifiers, and particles.

VOWEL-SHORTENING SYMBOL WITH แ- AND -อ

แข็ง	/khěŋ/ to be hard, firm, strong
แขยัก	/khàjèg, kha-/ bit by bit (of climbing)
แจ็ด	/chéd/ bright (red) (restricted mod.)
แด็กแด้	/dègdêɛ/ chrysalis. Also ดักแด้ /dàgdêɛ/.
ก็	/kɔ̂ʔ, kɔ̂-/ then, consequently, also
	Always spelled without vowel, as shown. A very common and important word.
หร็อก	/rɔ̂g/ (emphatic particle). Also หรอก but with same pronunciation.
หร็อมแหร็ม	/rɔ̂mrěm/ sparsely
หย็อกหย็อย	/jɔ̂gjɔ̌j/ disheveled, mussed (as hair)

5. The Tonal Markers and Vowel Length

Since the vowel-shortening symbol $\overset{\centerdot}{-}$ cannot be employed with the vowels เ–, แ– and –อ when a tonal marker is also required in the writing of the syllable (p. 69), there is no way within the conventional writing system to distinguish short /-e-/, /-ɛ-/ and /-ɔ-/ from long /-ee-/, /-ɛɛ-/ and /-ɔɔ-/ if tonal markers are used. All that can be done is to make a few very general statements which may be helpful to the foreign student of Thai. These are as follows:

1. The vowel เ– plus any one of the four tonal markers is normally read short, e.g.

THE VOWEL เ– WITH TONAL MARKERS

เก่ง	/kèŋ/ to be expert (in), good (at)
เบ่ง	/bèŋ/ to expand
เช่น	/chên/ such as
เล่น	/lên/ to play
เร่ว	/rêw/ cardamom
เว้น	/wén/ to omit, except
เม้ม	/mém/ to compress (e.g. the lips)
เจ๊ง	/céŋ/ to go bankrupt (< Chin.)
เป๊ง	/pěŋ/ strictly, sharp (as "noon sharp")
โกร่งเกร่ง	/krɔ̌oŋkrěeŋ/ to be sparse; sparsely, few

An exception. Note the difference between the last two examples. The long /-ee-/ can be predicted, however, because of the unambiguous long /-oo-/ in the first of the two ablaut reduplicated syllables.

2A. The vowels แ– and –อ are usually, but not in-
variably, short under the low tone in live syllables,
e.g.

THE VOWELS แ– AND –อ WITH MARKED LOW TONE

แจ่ม	/cɛ̀m/ to be clear
แบ่ง	/bɛ̀ŋ/ to divide (up)
แผ่น	/phɛ̀n/ Clf. for sheets (as of paper)
แหม่ม	/mɛ̀m/ Occidental woman (< Eng.)
แห่ง	/hɛ̀ŋ/ place; Clf. for places
ส่อง	/sɔ̀ŋ/ to shine
หม่อม	/mɔ̀m/ (title for descendants of roy.)
บ่อย	/bɔ̀j/ to be often
หน่อย	/nɔ̀j/ a little bit. Also /nɔ̀ɔj/.
ก่อน	/kɔ̀ɔn/ before

2B. The vowels แ– and –อ are either short or long
(depending upon the word) under the falling tone in
live syllables, e.g.

THE VOWELS แ– AND –อ WITH MARKED FALLING TONE

แข้ง	/khɛ̂ŋ/ shin
แกล้ง	/klɛ̂ɛŋ/ to make a show of, pretense of
แล่น	/lɛ̂n/ to run (of a boat)
แป้น	/pɛ̂n/ (name for a woman)
แป้ง	/pɛ̂ɛŋ/ powder (face powder), flour
แห้ว	/hɛ̂w/ water chestnut
แก้ว	/kɛ̂w/ crystal. Sometimes /kɛ̂ɛw/.
ต้อง	/tɔ̂ŋ/ to have to, must
ห้อง	/hɔ̂ŋ/ room

ห้อย   /hɔ̂j/ to hang (down)

 อ้อย   /ʔɔ̂j/ sugar cane

2C. The vowels แ– and –อ are always long under
the high tone in live syllables, e.g.

THE VOWELS แ– AND –อ WITH MARKED HIGH TONE

แล้ง   /lɛ́ɛŋ/ to be dry (as of the season)

แล้ว   /lɛ́ɛw/ already

ร้อย   /rɔ́ɔj/ hundred

ร้อน   /rɔ́ɔn/ to be hot

ช้อน   /chɔ́ɔn/ spoon

2D. The vowels แ– and –อ are usually short under
the rising tone in those syllables where it is marked
by the use of the 4th tonal marker, but such usage
is in any case rare. (High consonants in live syllables indicate a rising tone when no tonal marker is
used, and these consonants will take ⁓ if the vowel
is to be read short; see examples on p. 72). Examples
in which the 4th tonal marker is used are:

THE VOWELS แ– AND –อ WITH MARKED RISING TONE

แจ๋ว   /cɛ̌w/ crystal (clear)(restricted mod.)

กระป๋อง   /kràpɔ̌ŋ, kra-/ (tin-)can

กร๋อกกร๋อย   /krɔ̌gkrɔ̌j/ very humble, poor

3. In dead syllables marked tones are always rare
and unusual no matter what the vowel may be. When the
vowel is ิ–, แ– or –อ the reading is most often short
in dead syllables, but in a few instances the reading
is long. Most words coming in this category are recent
loanwords from Chinese or English.

เจ๊ก	/cég/ Chinese (informal term)(< Chin.)
แก๊บ	/kɛ́b/ cap (< Eng.)
แก๊ส	/kɛ́ɛɑ ~ kɛ́ɛs/ gas (< Eng.)
แจ๊ด	/cɛ́d/ bright (red)(restricted mod.)
ก๊อก	/kɔ́g/ (water) faucet (< Eng. "cock")
ชอก, ช๊อก	/chɔ́g/ chalk (< Eng.)
ล๊อกแล๊ก	/lɔ́glɛ̂g/ to be inattentive, shifty

This word uses the 1st tonal marker specifically to indicate that the vowels are short. If no tonal marker were used the tone would be the same but the vowels would be read long.

6. Irregular Readings for Vowel Lengths

There are various types of special cases in which a short vowel is read long or a long vowel is read short. A brief description of the most important of these is provided in this section.

A. Lengthened Vowels

(1) There is a tendency to lengthen a short vowel under the high tone in live syllables, particularly in the case of those written with the symbols $-้า$, l$-้า$, $\text{ใ}-$, and $\text{ไ}-$ (i.e. the vowel + sonorant symbols, p. 14). Some of the words coming in this category are read with a long vowel in final position (alone or in compounds), with a short vowel in nonfinal position (in compounds), e.g.

$-้า$	น้ำ	/náam/ water
	ห้องน้ำ	/hɔ̂ŋnáam/ bathroom
	น้ำแข็ง	/námkhɛ̌ŋ/ ice

เ–า	เช้า	/cháaw/	to be early (in the morning)
	เท้า	/tháaw/	foot (elegant)
ไ–	ไม้	/máaj/	stick, wood
	ต้นไม้	/tônmáaj/	tree
	ไม้ขีดไฟ	/májkhìidfaj/	a match
	ไม้ตรี	/májtrii/	the 3rd tonal marker
ใ–	ใช้	/cháaj ~ cháj/	to use ...; to be used

(2) The vowel + sonorant symbol เ–า is sometimes lengthened under the falling tone, sometimes not. Note the readings given in the following set of words:

เจ้า   /câaw/ Lord, royal person, prince

But sometimes also spelled จ้าว.

หม่อมเจ้า   /mɔ̀mcâaw/ royal grandchildren

But may sometimes be read /mɔ̀mcâw/ if used as a title immediately preceding the given name of the royal personage having the title.

เจ้า   /câw/ you (superior sp. to inferior)

เจ้า   /câw-/ master, owner (see ex. below)

เจ้าของ   /câwkhɔ̌ɔŋ/ master, owner

(3) One word spelled with เ–า under the low tone is <u>always</u> read with a long vowel, viz.

เปล่า   /plàaw/ to be empty, blank, plain; in vain; no!

B. Shortened Vowels

(1) The symbol เ–ิ/ is normally read long. In at least two instances, however, it is read short, viz.

เงิน   /ŋən/ silver; money

เจิ่ง   /cə̀ŋ/ to be inundated

(2) At least two words spelled with —า under the falling tone are normally read short, viz.

ท่าน /thân/ you; he, she, they (sp. of elders or superiors)

อ้าย /ʔâj/ Derogatory or insulting title used before first names of men

(3) S̆everal words shorten the vowel of a middle-toned syllable —ยา— when it is in penultimate position. But the words are also sometimes read with a half-long vowel. This is shown by placing the second of the two a's in parentheses in the phonetic transscription, e.g.

วิทยาลัย   /wídthája(a)laj, -tha-/ college

วิทยาศาสตร์ /wídthája(a)sàad, -tha-/ science

พยายาม   /phája(a)jaam, pha-/ to try, attempt

โรงพยาบาล /rooŋphája(a)baan, -pha-/ hospital

7. Irregular Readings for Tones

There are a few disyllabic words which have an irregular reading for the tone of their second syllable. All such syllables are "dead" syllables (see p. 26) beginning in a sonorant, and their tones are read as if the sonorant were governed by a preceding MIDDLE or HIGH consonant. In these cases it is the preceding syllable which begins in a MIDDLE or HIGH consonant and this, in effect, governs the tone of its own syllable and the syllable following. But this type of situation is not a regular one.

The pronunciation and spelling of the following words must therefore be memorized, especially since the pronunciation of most of them is incorrectly marked in McFarland's Thai-English Dictionary, a

source which is in most other respects a useful one
for the relatively advanced student of THAI.

IRREGULAR TONES: LOW INSTEAD OF FALLING

ประโยชน์   /pràjòod, pra- / usefulness, advantage

ประโยค   /pràjòog, pra- / sentence (grammar)

ประมาท   /pràmàad, pra- / to be negligent

ตำรวจ   /tamrùad/ the police

สำรวจ   /sămrùad/ to explore, survey

IRREGULAR TONES: LOW INSTEAD OF HIGH

ประวัติ   /pràwàd, pra-/ description, history

ประวัติศาสตร์ /pràwàdtìsàad, pra-/ history (subject)

ดำริ   /damrí?/ to consider (royal, elegant)

ดำรัส   /damràd/ to speak; speech (royal)

สำเร็จ   /sămrèd/ to be finished, complete,
          successful

In addition to the examples cited above many
recent loanwords from English have irregular pronunciation as to tones.

8. Ambiguities

Certain features of the Thai writing system give
rise to ambiguities, i.e. the same sequence of symbols may have more than one pronunciation or more
than one possible pronunciation. Some of the more
common ambiguities are discussed below.

(1) When the complex vowel symbol เ—า has two
consonants between its two parts, it cannot be distinguished from a sequence C + /-ee/ followed by
C + /-aa/. Homographs are rare, but the proper reading for all such combinations must be learned, e.g.

เสลา   /sàlǎw, sa-/ a kind of tree

    (or)   /sěelaa/ stone, mountain

เพลา   /phlaw/ axle

    (or)   /pheelaa/ time (literary)

(2) When the preposed vowel symbols เ–, แ– and
โ– are followed by ห plus a sonorant, it is impossible
to tell whether the ห is ห นำ or the initial pronounced consonant ห followed by a final consonant.
That is, this is true if no tonal marker is required,
e.g.

แหน   /něɛ/ duckweed

    (or)   /hěɛn/ to be solicitous about

แหม   /měɛ/ Oh! (interjection)

เหม   /hěem/ gold (literary)

But if a tonal marker is required it will be placed
over the sonorant if the ห is ห นำ (first example below), and over ห if the sonorant is the syllable final (second example below).

แหง   /ŋèɛ/ to be small, little, young

แหง   /hèŋ/ place, location

(3) If the symbol ว occurs between two consonants
it is usually to be read as /-ua-/. But sometimes it
is to be read as syllable initial /w-/, though this
latter reading is extremely rare. Moreover, if the
first of the two consonants is ห, the ห may be either
the initial pronounced consonant or ห นำ. Examples:

สวน   /sǔan/ garden

สวง   /sàwǒŋ, sa-/ (first name for a man)

ควร	/khuan/ ought to, should
(or)	/kháwɔɔn, kha-/ (as in the ex. below)
รังควร	/raŋkháwɔɔn, -kha-/ (a surname)
บวม	/buam/ to swell, be swollen
บวร	/bɔɔwɔɔn, bɔ-/ (a surname)
หวง	/hŭaŋ/ to keep for oneself, be jealous of
(or)	/wŏŋ/ (short form of สิวง, man's name)

(4) If the symbol อ occurs between two consonants it is usually to be read /-ɔɔ-/. But in a few rare instances it must be read as syllable initial /ʔ-/.

ผอม	/phɔ̌ɔm/ to be thin, lean, skinny
(or)	/phàʔom, pha-/ (as in the ex. below)
ผอิดผอม	/phàʔʸ̀ydphàʔom, pha-..-pha-/ reluctant to speak
ผอบ	/phàʔòb, pha-/ small container with a triangular lid

9. Recent Changes in Spelling

A few minor changes in spelling were introduced in the 1950 ed. of the official Thai Dictionary put out under the auspices of the Ministry of Education. Current newspapers and recently issued books use the new spelling. But the McFarland Thai-English Dictionary, commonly used by foreign students of Thai, was published prior to the time these changes were introduced and a recent reissue of this work (1954) has no corrections in the text because it was done by the photographic process. Therefore a student who tries to read a current Thai newspaper with the aid of the McFarland dictionary will have difficulty in locating some of the words unless he takes into account the points discussed below.

(1) The vowel —ะ has been dropped in the spelling of many common words, e.g.

New Way	Old Way	Transcription	
ฉบับ	ฉะบับ	/chàbàb, cha-/	issue, copy
เฉพาะ	ฉะเพาะ	/chàphɔ́ʔ, cha-/	to be particular to
ชนะ	ชะนะ	/chánáʔ, cha-/	to win
ชนิก	ชะนิก	/cháníd, cha-/	kind, sort, variety
พม่า	พะม่า	/phámâa, pha-/	Burma; Burmese

But many other words still retain the vowel —ะ, e.g.

มะลิ	/málíʔ, ma-/	jasmine
ระยะ	/rájáʔ, ra-/	distance
ทะเล	/thálee, tha-/	sea

(2) Some simplification in the writing of final consonant clusters has been introduced in some words, e.g.

New Way	Old Way	Transcription	
เขต	เขตต์	/khèed/	limit, boundary
กิจ	กิจจ์	/kìd/	activity
วุฒ	วุฑฒ์	/wúd/	to grow, increase (literary)

(3) A very few words formerly spelled with ไ— for /-aj/ are now spelled —ัย. An important example is:

New Way	Old Way	Transcription	
ตรัย	ไตร	/traj/	three (literary, special)

But the old spelling is still used in some contexts. The new spelling is used especially in Buddhist contexts, as in the example below.

รัตนตรัย	/rádtànátraj, -tana-/ the Three Gems (of Buddhism)

CHAPTER VII

N U M E R A L S   A N D   S P E C I A L   S I G N S

1. Numerals

The so-called Arabic numerals used in Europe and
in America are ultimately derived from the ancient
Hindu numerals. The Thai numerals have the same origin, but the Thai obtained them as a part of their
total writing system complex which is derived from
the Devanagari (p. 1). The actual numerals with
their names are listed below.

THAI NUMERALS

๑	1	หนึ่ง	/nỳŋ/ one
๒	2	สอง	/sɔ̌ɔŋ/ two
๓	3	สาม	/sǎam/ three
๔	4	สี่	/sìi/ four
๕	5	ห้า	/hâa/ five
๖	6	หก	/hòg/ six
๗	7	เจ็ก	/cèd/ seven
๘	8	แปก	/pὲɛd/ eight
๙	9	เก้า	/kâw/ nine
๐	0	ศูนย์	/sǔun/ zero

The basic rule for making these symbols is the same as that for making the consonants. In other words, one starts out by first making the little circle in ๑, ๒, ๓, etc. The pen then moves to the right or the left (or right, then left) as demanded by the nature of the symbol. The symbol for "9" is made in two strokes, viz. ๏ followed by ๘ giving ๙. The remaining symbols are made without lifting the pen from beginning to end. Note that the Thai zero is a small circle, not a small oval as is our Arabic zero.

The Thai numeral system is a decimal one and the higher numbers are formed by the use of the zero and the digits exactly as in our own system, viz.

๑๐	10	สิบ	/sìb/
๑๑	11	สิบเอ็ด	/sìbʔèd/
๑๕	15	สิบห้า	/sìbhâa/
๒๐	20	ยี่สิบ	/jîisìb/
๓๐	30	สามสิบ	/sǎamsìb/
๔๐	40	สี่สิบ	/sìisìb/
๑๐๐	100	หนึ่งร้อย	/nỳŋrɔ́ɔj/
๑๐๑	101	ร้อยเอ็ด	/rɔ́ɔjʔèd/
๓๔๕	345	สามร้อยสี่สิบห้า	/sǎamrɔ́ɔj sìisìbhâa/
๑๐๐๐	1000	หนึ่งพัน	/nỳŋphan/
๓๐๗๘	3078	สามพันเจ็ดสิบแปด	/sǎamphan cèdsìb- pɛ̀ɛd/
๔๕๙๖	4596	สี่พันห้าร้อยเก้าสิบหก	/sìiphan hâarɔ́ɔj kâwsìbhòg/

๑๐,๐๐๐	10,000	หนึ่งหมื่น /nɯ̀ŋmɯ̀ɯn/
๔๕,๒๐๐	45,200	สี่หมื่นห้าพันสองร้อย
		/sìimɯ̀ɯn hâaphan sɔ̌ɔŋrɔ́ɔj/
๑๐๐,๐๐๐	100,000	หนึ่งแสน /nɯ̀ŋsɛ̌ɛn/
๑๙๘,๐๐๐	198,000	หนึ่งแสนเก้าหมื่นแปดพัน
		/nɯ̀ŋsɛ̌ɛn kâwmɯ̀ɯn pɛ̀ɛdphan/
๑,๐๐๐,๐๐๐	1,000,000	หนึ่งล้าน /nɯ̀ŋláan/
๑๐,๐๐๐,๐๐๐	10,000,000	สิบล้าน (or) หนึ่งโกฏิ
		/sìbláan/ (or) /nɯ̀ŋkòod/

But /kòod/ is not used in reading higher numbers; see the example below.

๑๓๐,๐๐๐,๐๐๐	130,000,000	หนึ่งร้อยสามสิบล้าน
		/nɯ̀ŋrɔ́ɔj sǎamsìbláan/

~~~~~~

Our own Arabic numerals are also sometimes used in Thai books at the present time (see pp. 95 and 102), even though all the other writing may be in the conventional Thai orthography. Thai schoolchildren often learn their arithmetic by the use of Arabic numerals. They also, of course, learn to use their own numerals as well.

2. Typographical Signs

Both traditional typographical signs and many additional signs recently borrowed from the West are to be found in modern Thai books and newspapers. Traditional signs still in common use are listed on the following page with their names and examples.

TYPOGRAPHICAL SIGNS

ๆ	ไม้ยมก	/májjámóg, -ja-/ the repeat sign, e.g.
อื่น ๆ		/ʔỳynʔỳyn/ other, others
ช้า ๆ		/cháacháa/ slowly

~~~~~~

ฯ	ไปยาลน้อย	/pajjaannɔ́ɔj/ used to indicate that a familiar, well-understood word or group of words has been omitted in writing. In reading, the omitted word or words must be supplied, e.g.
	กรุงเทพฯ	Stands for กรุงเทพมหานคร /kruŋthêeb máhǎanákhɔɔn, ma-..-na-/ (the Thai name for Bangkok). This name is always written with this symbol.
	นายกฯ	Stands for นายกรัฐมนตรี /naajóg rádthàmontrii, -tha-/ the premier

~~~~~~

ฯลฯ	ไปยาล่ใหญ่	/pajjaanjàj/ used like Eng. "etc." and read as /láʔ/ in a text. See example on p. 91.

~~~~~~

Additional typographical signs recently borrowed from the West are the following:

มหัพภาค	/máhàbphâag, ma-/ the period. Used in writing abbreviations (pp. 93-100), e.g.
น.	Abbrev. for นาฬิกา /naalíkaa/ "o'clock" (for time on the 24-hour basis).
ร.ร.	Abbrev. for โรงเรียน /rooŋrian/ "school."

~~~~~~

๙ุก	/cùd/ "dot, point." I.e., the dot used in writing decimals, e.g.
๘.๓๐ น.	8:30 A.M.
๒.๕๐	2.50. Read /sɔ̌ɔŋ cùd hâasìb/.

~~~~~~

๙ุกลูกน้ำ	/cùdlûugnáam/ the comma. Used in writing larger numbers, e.g.
๑๐,๐๐๐	10,000

~~~~~~

– ขีด	/khìid/ the dash. Sometimes not read, e.g.
เด็ก ๔ – ๕ คน	/dèg sìi hâakhon/ "four (or) five children"
	But sometimes read as:
ถึง	/thʉ̌ŋ/ "to, up to, until," e.g.
๘.๔๕ – ๙.๐๐ น.	8:45 to 9:00 A.M.

~~~~~~

% เครื่องหมายร้อยละ	/khrʉ̂aŋmǎaj rɔ́ɔjlá?/ "per cent sign"
	But read as:
เปอร์เซ็นต์	/pəəsen/ "per cent" (< Eng.), e.g.
๑๐%	/sìb pəəsen/ 10%

~~~~~~

? เครื่องหมายคำถาม	/khrʉ̂aŋmǎaj khamthǎam/ "question mark," e.g.
เรียนไปทำไม?	/rian paj thammaj/ "Why study?"

~~~~~~

! อัศเจรีย์ /ʔàdsàceerii, -sa-/ the exclamation point. Also called:

เครื่องหมายตกใจ /khrŷaŋmǎaj tògcaj/ "the sign of being frightened"

Used with interjections and with exclamatory sentences, e.g.

อย่าตกใจ! /jàa tògcaj/ "Don't be scared!"

〜〜〜〜〜〜〜〜〜〜〜〜〜〜〜〜〜〜〜〜〜〜〜〜〜〜〜〜〜〜〜〜

" " เครื่องหมายคำพูด /khrŷaŋmǎaj khamphûud/ quotation marks ("spoken word symbols"). Additional terms for "open quotes" and "close quotes" are also used and are formed by adding the terms /pə̀əd/ "to open" and /pìd/ "to close," viz.

เครื่องหมายคำพูดเปิด open quotes

เครื่องหมายคำพูดปิด close quotes

Quotation marks are used to enclose direct quotations, e.g.

"ไม่ใช่ครับ" /mâjchâj khráb/ "No." (man speaking)

They are also used with proper names to indicate that the name is a pen name, e.g.

โดย "แสงทอง" /dooj sɛ̌ɛŋthɔɔŋ/ By "Saengthǫng."

〜〜〜〜〜〜〜〜〜〜〜〜〜〜〜〜〜〜〜〜〜〜〜〜〜〜〜〜〜〜〜〜

( ) วงเล็บ /woŋléb/ parentheses

Used to enclose parenthetical matter, usually of an explanatory nature, e.g.

กัมพูชา (เขมร) /kamphuuchaa (khàmě̌en)/ Cambodia (Khmer)

〜〜〜〜〜〜〜〜〜〜〜〜〜〜〜〜〜〜〜〜〜〜〜〜〜〜〜〜〜〜〜〜

3. Spaces and Other Punctuation

Thai words are not written with spaces between
them as is done in writing English and other European languages. All words within a phrase or clause
(or within a sentence containing a single clause)
are written together without any spacing, as is cus-
tomary in writing Sanskrit and other languages using
the Devanagari or one of its derivatives. Example:

ประเทศไทยตั้งอยู่ทางทิศตะวันออกเฉียงใต้ของทวีปเอเชีย

/prathêedthaj tâŋ jùu thaaŋ thídtawan?ɔ̀ɔg-
chiaŋtâj khɔ̌ɔŋ thawiib?eesia./

Thailand is situated in the southeast of the
continent of Asia. THAI READER, p. 185.

Spaces, on the other hand, set off the end of a
phrase, clause, or sentence and are therefore used
in places where we normally use the comma and the
period, e.g.

ไม่มีหิมะในประเทศไทย แต่มีลูกเห็บบ้างบางแห่ง ต้นไม้
เขียวและดอกไม้บานตลอดปี

/mâjmii hìmá? naj prathêedthaj, tɛ̀ɛ mii
lûughèb bâaŋ baaŋhὲŋ. tônmáaj khiaw lέ?
dɔ̀ɔgmáaj baan talɔ̀ɔd pii./

There is no snow in Thailand, but there is
some hail in some places. The trees are green
and the flowers bloom throughout the year.
THAI READER, p. 150.

Thai printed matter (as opposed to typewritten
matter) is arranged so that the righthand margin is

even, just as is done in our own printed books. But
in Thai this can mean that the end of a sentence is
unmarked in any way. If the end of the sentence is
flush with the righthand margin, there will be no
special mark to set it off as the end of a sentence.
Contrariwise, in order to adjust the righthand margin the printer will sometimes insert an extra space
or two which is not meant to be interpreted as the
end of a phrase or clause. In the beginning these
things will be a bit confusing to the student, but
after he has had a little practice in reading he
will become accustomed to them.

Spaces are also used to set off words in a series,
and this furnishes still another instance in which a
space corresponds to our comma, e.g.

สินค้าสำคัญของประเทศไทยมี ข้าว ไม้สัก   ยาง   หมู
วัว ปลา   และแร่ต่าง ๆ

/sǐnkháa sǎmkhan khɔ̌ɔŋ prathêedthaj mii,

khâaw, májsàg, jaaŋ, mǔu, wua, plaa lɛ́ʔ rɛ̂ɛ

tàaŋtàaŋ./

The important products of Thailand are rice,
teak, rubber, hogs, cattle, fish, and various ores. THAI READER, p. 158.

Spaces also have other conventional uses in written Thai, viz. (1) between the first and last names
of people (but not between a title like "Mr." and
the first name), e.g.

พ่อของเขาชื่อนายขาบ รักไทย

/phɔ̂ɔ khɔ̌ɔŋkhǎw chŷy naajkhàab rágthaj./

His father's name is Mr. Khap Rakthai. THAI
READER, p. 76.

(2) before and after numerals, e.g.

พ่อค้าช้างผู้หนึ่งได้วัดช้างถึง ๒๐๐๐ ตัว มีตัวเดียวที่สูง
ถึง ๕ ฟุต ๔ นิ้ว

/phɔ̂ɔkháacháaŋ phûunỳŋ dâjwád cháaŋ thỳŋ

sɔ̌ɔŋphan tua, mii tuadiaːw thâwnán thîi sǔuŋ

thỳŋ kâwfúd sìiníw./

An elephant merchant measured up to 2000 ele-
phants, (and) there was only one which reached
the height of 9 feet, 4 inches.   "SCIENCE,"
vol. 5, pp. 323-324.

(3) before and after the repeat sign, e.g.

ทางเหนือของประเทศไทยมีภูเขาสูง ๆ มาก

/thaaŋ nỳa khɔ̌ɔŋ prathêedthaj mii phuukhǎw

sǔuŋsǔuŋ mâag./

In the north of Thailand there are many quite
high mountains.   THAI READER, p. 163.

(4) before and after ๆลๆ, e.g.

ประเทศไทยส่ง ข้าว ดีบุก ๆลๆ ไปขายต่างประเทศ

/prathêedthaj sòŋ khâaw, diibùg láʔ, pajkhǎaj

tàaŋprathêed./

Thailand exports rice, tin, etc.

(5) before and after parentheses, e.g.

คนนำทางกะว่ามันสูงราว ๕ – ๕ ศอก (ราว ๑๒ – ๑๔ ฟุต)

/khonnamthaaŋ kà? wâa man sǔuŋ raaw pɛ̀ɛd kâw-

sɔ̀ɔg (raaw sìbsɔ̌ɔŋ thǔ̌ŋ sìbsìi fúd)./·

The guide guessed it was around 8-9 forearm
lengths (around 12-14 feet) in height.
"SCIENCE," vol. 5, p. 326.

If, upon reaching the righthand margin, the typ-
ist or printer finds it necessary to break into the
middle of a word, a hyphen is often used, just as in
our own typed or printed matter, e.g.

กรุงเทพฯเป็นจุดรวมของการคมนาคม   มีทางรถ—
ไฟ และทางรถยนต์   จากกรุงเทพฯไปยังเมืองต่าง ๆ
ทั่วประเทศ

/kruŋthêeb pen cùdruam khɔ̌ɔŋ kaankhommanaakhom.

mii thaaŋródfaj lɛ́? thaaŋródjon càag kruŋthêeb

paj jaŋ myaŋ tâaŋtâaŋ thûa prathêed./

Bangkok is the center of communication. There
are railways and highways from Bangkok to the
different towns all over the country.   THAI
READER, p. 161.

The remaining types of punctuation marks are used
very much as they are in English books. Quotation
marks set off direct quotations, and the question
mark and exclamation point designate questions and
exclamations, respectively (see pp. 87-88). In addition, paragraphs are indented as in our own books.

4. Abbreviations

Abbreviations of certain common words are sometimes used in modern written Thai. They are always
set off by the use of a period. Sometimes the first
consonant of the word is used in abbreviation, e.g.

น.　　นาฬิกา.　　　/naalíkaa/ o'clock (of time
　　　　　　　　　　　on the 24-hour basis)

At other times the first consonant of each of two
parts of a word will be used as the abbreviation,
and in this event there is usually a period after
each of the two consonants, e.g.

น.ร.　　นักเรียน　　　/nágrian/ student

But if the first consonant of either syllable　is
ห นำ this letter will be skipped in favor of　the
second consonant of the syllable, e.g.

ก.ม.　　กฎหมาย　　　/kòdmǎaj/ law

The reason for this is that ห นำ must be used　in
front of all sonorants to convert them to the HIGH
series and it is therefore not a sufficiently dis-
tinctive letter to be used for purposes of abbreviation.

Certain standard abbreviations transliterated
from European languages may have a period following
only the last consonant of the abbreviation.　But
sometimes even these abbreviations will be written
with two periods, e.g.

กม. (or) ก.ม. กิโลเมตร /kìloomét/ kilometer (km.)

In rarer instances the first two or three letters
of a word, including perhaps a vowel, are used in
abbreviation, e.g.

โทร.　　โทรศัพท์　　　/thoorásàb/ telephone

Some of the more commonly used abbreviations are listed and explained below. But certain other specialized categories of abbreviations are discussed in later sections (pp. 96-101).

TITLES

ม.จ.   หม่อมเจ้า /mɔ̀mcâw, -câaw/ M.C. (a title for those in the grandchild generation of royal descent, or treated as such)

Higher titles are normally not subject to abbreviation.

ม.ร.ว.   หม่อมราชวงศ์ /mɔ̀mrâadcháwoŋ, -cha-/ M.R. (a title for those in the great-grandchild generation of royal descent, or treated as such), e.g.

ม.ร.ว. เสนี ปราโมช   /mɔ̀mrâadchawoŋ sěenii praamôod/ M.R. Seni Pramot

ม.ล.   หม่อมหลวง /mɔ̀mlǔaŋ/ M.L. (a title for those in the great-great-grandchild generation of royal descent, or treated as such)

น.ส.   นางสาว /naaŋsǎaw/ "Miss," e.g.

น.ส. ศรี ภักดี   /naaŋsǎaw sǐi phágdii/ Miss Si Phakdi

But the titles นาย /naaj/ "Mr." and นาง /naaŋ/ "Mrs." are not subject to abbreviation.

ดร.   Transliterated from the English abbreviation "Dr." and read as /dɔ́gtə̀ə/, e.g.

ดร. ราลฟ์ บันช์   Dr. Ralph Bunche

Additional miscellaneous abbreviations commonly seen in newspapers are listed on the following page.

ก.พ.　คณะกรรมการข้าราชการพลเรือน　/khaná?
kammakaan khâarâadchakaanphonlaryan/
Civil Service

ส.ส.　สมาชิกสภาผู้แทนราษฎร　/samaachíg saphaa-
phûuthɛɛn râadsadɔɔn/ Member of Par-
liament

ค.ร.ม.　คณะรัฐมนตรี　/khaná? rádthamontrii/ the
cabinet (of ministers of state)

ร.ม.ต.　รัฐมนตรี　/rádthamontrii/ minister (of
state)

ร.ฟ.ท.　รถไฟไทย　/ródfajthaj/ Thai Railways

Formerly called /ródfajlǔaŋ/ "Royal
State Railways" and abbrev. as ร.ฟ.ถ.

ก.ม.　กฎหมาย /kòdmǎaj/ law. Sometimes also
the abbrev. for "kilometer" (p. 93).

จ.ม.　จดหมาย /còdmǎaj/ letter (epistle)

ป.บ.　ไปรษณียบัตร /prajsaniijabàd/ post card

ป.ล.　ปฏิลิขิต /pàti? líkhìd/ postscript, P.S.

น.ร.　นักเรียน /nágrian/ student (in school)

ร.ร.　โรงเรียน /rooŋrian/ school

ร.ง.　โรงงาน /rooŋŋaan/ factory

โทร.　โทรศัพท์ /thoorasàb/ telephone. Used in
front of telephone numbers (either
Thai or Arabic numerals), e.g.

โทร. ๑๐๖๕๔ /thoorasàb nɯ̀ŋ sǔun hòg hâa sìi/

โทร. 10654　Tel. 10654

น.　นาฬิกา /naalíkaa/ o'clock (of time on
the 24-hour basis), e.g.

๐๒.๐๐ น.　/sɔ̌ɔŋ naalíkaa/ 2 A.M.

๒๐.๐๐ น.　/jîisìb naalíkaa/ 8 P.M.

สต.　สตางค์ /sataaŋ/ satang, 1-100th of a
baht, e.g.

๒๕ สต.　/jîisìbhâa sataaŋ/ 25 satangs

บ.	บาท	/bàad/ baht, tical
จ.ว.	จังหวัด	/caŋwàd/ čhangwat, province
อ.	อำเภอ	/ʔamphəə/ amphoe, district

5. Metric System Abbreviations

The commonly used abbreviations for the units of the metric system have been transliterated from the standard European abbreviations as shown below.

METRIC SYSTEM ABBREVIATIONS

ก.	กรัม	/kram/ gram (g.)
ดคก.	เดคากรัม	/deekhaakram/ decagram (dkg.)
ฮก.	เฮกโตกรัม	/hégtookram/ hectogram (hg.)
กก.	กิโลกรัม	/kìlookram/ kilogram (kg.)
ดก.	เดซิกรัม	/deesíkram/ decigram (dg.)
ซก.	เซ็นติกรัม	/sentìkram/ centigram (cg.)
มก.	มิลลิกรัม	/minlíkram/ milligram (mg.)
ม.	เมตร	/méd/ meter (m.)
ดคม.	เดคาเมตร	/deekhaaméd/ decameter (dkm.)
ฮม.	เฮกโตเมตร	/hégtooméd/ hectometer (hm.)
กม.	กิโลเมตร	/kìlooméd/ kilometer (km.). Sometimes also abbrev. as ก.ม. (p. 93).
ดม.	เดซิเมตร	/deesíméd/ decimeter (dm.)
ซม.	เซ็นติเมตร	/sentìméd/ centimeter (cm.)
มม.	มิลลิเมตร	/minlíméd/ millimeter (mm.)
ล.	ลิตร	/líd/ liter (l.)
ดคล.	เดคาลิตร	/deekhaalíd/ decaliter (dkl.)

ฮล	เฮกโตลิตร	/hégtoolíd/	hectoliter (hl.)
กล.	กิโลลิตร	/kìloolíd/	kiloliter (kl.)
ดล.	เดซิลิตร	/deesílíd/	deciliter (dl.)
ซล.	เซ็นติลิตร	/sentílíd/	centiliter (cl.)
มล.	มิลลิลิตร	/minlílíd/	milliliter (ml.)

6. Thai Initials and European Initials

The consonant letters of the Thai alphabet can be used as initials, i.e., as abbreviations of personal names. When so used the letters are always followed by a period, e.g.

ก.	/kɔɔ/ Abbreviation for any name beginning in ก.
ข.	/khɔ̌ɔ/ Abbreviation for any name beginning in ข, e.g.
ข. ภักดี	/khɔ̌ɔ phágdii/ where /khɔ̌ɔ/ could be the abbreviation for ขาบ /khàab/ or any other name beginning in ข.
ค.	/khɔɔ/ Abbreviation for any name beginning in ค.

Etc.

The letters of the English alphabet are also used as abbreviations, particularly for expressions like "DDT," "Vitamin 'A,'" etc. They are also used in the transliteration of initials of American, British and other European personal names. The letters of the English alphabet are written out in Thai according to the pronunciation used for the letters of the alphabet in British English. A period is then placed at the end in order to show that these are abbreviations. The convention (or conventions) for writing these letters is shown on the following page.

LETTERS OF THE ENGLISH ALPHABET

เอ.	/ʔee/	A
บี.	/bii/	B
ซี.	/sii/	C
ดี.	/dii/	D
อี.	/ʔii/	E
เอฟ. เอ็ฟ.	/ʔéf/	F
ยี. จี.	/jii/ (or) /cii/	G
เอช. เอ็ช.	/ʔéch/	H
ไอ.	/ʔaj/	I
เจ.	/cee/	J
เค.	/khee/	K
เอล. เอ็ล. แอล.	/ʔel/ (or) /ʔɛl/	L
เอม. เอ็ม.	/ʔem/	M
เอน. เอ็น.	/ʔen/	N
โอ.	/ʔoo/	O
พี.	/phii/	P
คิว.	/khiw/	Q
อาร์.	/ʔaa/	R
เอส. เอ็ส.	/ʔés/	S
ที.	/thii/	T
ยู.	/juu/	U
วี.	/wii/	V
ดับเปิลยู. ดับบลิว.	/dàbbəljuu/ (or) /dàbbaliw/	W
เอกซ์. เอ็กซ์.	/ʔég/	X
วาย. ไวย์.	/waaj/ (or) /waj/	Y
เซ็ด. แซ็ด.	/sêd/ (or) /sêd/	Z, i.e. zed

Examples:

วิตามิน เอ.	/wítaamin ʔee/	Vitamin A
วิตามิน บี.	/wítaamin bii/	Vitamin B
ดี.ดี.ที.	/dii dii thii/	DDT
เอฟ.เอ.โอ.	/ʔéf ʔee ʔoo/	FAO
เอ็ช.ดับบลิว.วาร์ค	/ʔéch dàbbaliw wàad/	H. W. Ward

7. Dates

Thailand uses the Buddhist era, reckoned from
the date of the death of the Buddha, for all official purposes. Different Buddhist countries have
slightly different dates for this event, but in
Thailand it is reckoned to be 543 years before the
beginning of the Christian era.

To determine the year according to the Christian
era, subtract 543 from the year of the Buddhist era.
To determine the year according to the Buddhist era,
add 543 to the year of the Christian era.

The abbreviations used for these two eras of time
reckoning are shown and illustrated below.

พ.ศ.	พุทธศักราช	/phúdthasàŋkaràad/ Buddhist era, i.e. B.E., e.g.
พ.ศ. ๒๔๙๘		/phúdthasàŋkaràad sɔ̌ɔŋphan sìi-rɔ́ɔj kâwsìbpèɛd/ 2498 B.E. (equivalent to 1955 A.D.)
ค.ศ.	คริสตศักราช	/khrídsàŋkaràad/ Christian era, i.e. A.D., e.g.
ค.ศ. ๑๙๕๕		/khrídsàŋkaràad nɯ̀ŋphan kâwrɔ́ɔj hâasìbhâa/ 1955 A.D. (equiva- lent to 2498 B.E.)

When dates are given in full the form used is
that given in the first line of Thai on the following
page. But sometimes the abbreviation for the era is

omitted (second line).

วันอาทิตย์ที่ ๑๗ ตุลาคม พ.ศ. ๒๔๙๗

วันอาทิตย์ที่ ๑๗ ตุลาคม ๒๔๙๗

/wan?aathíd thîisìbcèd tùlaakhom phúdthasàgkaràad
sɔ̌ɔŋphan sìirɔ̌ɔj kâwsìbcèd/ Sunday, Oct. 17, 2497 B.E.

Two sets of abbreviations for the names of the
months are shown below. Of these two the first is
perhaps the more commonly used.

ม.ค.	มกร.	มกราคม	/mógkaraakhom/ January
ก.พ.	กุมภ.	กุมภาพันธ์	/kumphaaphan/ February
มี.ค.	มีน.	มีนาคม	/miinaakhom/ March
ม.ย.	เมษ.	เมษายน	/meesǎajon/ April
พ.ค.	พฤษภ.	พฤษภาคม	/phrýdsaphaakhom, -ss-/ May
มิ.ย.	มิถุน.	มิถุนายน	/míthùnaajon/ June
ก.ค.	กรกฎ.	กรกฎาคม	/karágkadaakhom/ July
ส.ค.	สิงห.	สิงหาคม	/sǐŋhǎakhom/ August
ก.ย.	กันย.	กันยายน	/kan· .ajon/ September
ต.ค.	ตุล.	ตุลาคม	/ ˌlaakhom/ October
พ.ย.	พฤศจิก.	พฤศจิกายน	/phrýdsacikaajon, -ss-/ Nov.
ธ.ว.	ธันว.	ธันวาคม	/thanwaakhom/ December

Shortened forms of a date may be given in the
style shown below. The first line has the first type
of month abbreviation, the second line the second
type.

๒๖ ต.ค. ๒๔๙๘

๒๖ ธันว. ๒๔๙๘

/wanthíi jîisìbhòg thanwaakhom sɔ̌ɔŋphan sìirɔ́ɔj kâw-
sìbpɛ̀ɛd/ December 26, 2498 (B.E.)

In the most extreme shortened form of a date, the
month is referred to by its consecutive number and
the year date is shown by giving the last two numerals only. Observe that the first number stands for
the day of the month and the second number is the
number of the month (the style most frequently used
in Europe). This is in contrast to the style in
which the first number is the number of the month
and the second number is the day of the month (the
style most frequently used in America).

๒๖ / ๑๒ / ๕๕

26/12/98, i.e. 12-26-55 (in the American style and
using the Christian era in place of the Buddhist era)

8. Pagination

The pages of a modern Thai book or newspaper are
numbered in the same way that European and American
books are, but several styles of numbers may be used.

(1) Ordinary Thai numerals are used in the main
body of the book, e.g.

๑ ๒ ๓ ๔ ๕ ๖ ๗ ๘ ๙ ๑๐ ๑๑ ๑๒

The front matter of the book is paginated by the
use of the Thai letters of the alphabet in place
of the Roman numerals used in European books, e.g.

ก ข ค ฆ ง จ ฉ ช ซ

(2) Ordinary Thai numerals are used in the main
body of the book as above. The front matter is

paginated by the use of capital Roman numerals, e.g.

I   II   III   IV   V   VI   VII   VIII   IX   X

(3) The main body of the book is paginated by the use of Arabic numerals, e.g.

1   2   3   4   5   6   7   8   9   10   11   12

The four pages which follow contain samples of
Thai handwriting done by two different persons.
Three styles of handwriting are illustrated: precise, medium, and fast. Page 104 has a sample of
the precise style, and page 105 shows the same text
in both medium and fast styles. Pages 106 and 107
illustrate the medium and fast styles, respectively, of a second brief text. Both texts are taken
from the THAI READER. The first is the fourth paragraph of เรื่องประเทศไทย, pp. 185-187, but the date
is expanded to show both B.E. and A.D. The second
text is เรื่องรถ, pp. 45-46.

The style of lettering in precise handwriting
most closely resembles printing. The other two
styles have characteristics associated with handwriting only. A few examples selected to show some
of the peculiarities are given below.

–ะ	as in	ระยะ	ง:ย:	
–ั	as in	สำหรับ	สำหรับ	สำหรับ
–ั	as in	ทัน	ทัน	
–ั	as in	ปั้น	หนั	หนั
โ–	as in	โดย	โดย	โดย
ข	as in	ขี่	ข	
ร	as in	รถราง	รถราง	
ศ, ษ	as in	เศษ	เศษ	
ส	as in	สาม	สาม	

The student who is interested in the problem will be
able to find other examples on his own initiative.

กรุงเทพฯ เป็นเมืองหลวงของประเทศไทยตั้ง
แต่ พ.ศ. ๒๓๒๔ (ค.ศ. ๑๗๘๑) ตั้งอยู่บนฝั่ง
ตะวันออกของแม่น้ำเจ้าพระยา   เมืองสำคัญของ
ประเทศนอกจากกรุงเทพฯคืออยุธยา ตั้งอยู่เหนือ
กรุงเทพฯ   ตามฝั่งแม่น้ำเจ้าพระยา พิษณุโลก
ลำปาง และเชียงใหม่ เป็นเมืองใหญ่ทางภาคเหนือ
ทางภาคใต้มีเมืองใหญ่หลายเมืองเช่น เพชรบุรี
นครปฐม ราชบุรี สุราษฎร์ นครศรีธรรมราช
สงขลา ตรัง ภูเก็ต และ ปัตตานี

กรุงเทพฯ เป็นเมืองหลวงของประเทศไทย ตั้ง
แต่ พ.ศ. ๒๓๒๘ (ค.ศ. ๑๗๘๑) ตั้งอยู่บนฝั่งตะวัน
ออกของแม่น้ำเจ้าพระยา เมืองสำคัญของประเทศนอก
จากกรุงเทพฯคือ อยุธยา ตั้งอยู่เหนือกรุงเทพฯ. ตาม
ฝั่งแม่น้ำเจ้าพระยา พิษณุโลก ลำปาง และเชียง-
ใหม่ เป็นเมืองใหญ่ ทางภาคเหนือ ทางภาคใต้มี
เมืองใหญ่ หลายเมืองเช่น เพชรบุรี นครปฐม
ราชบุรี สุราษฎร์ นครศรีธรรมราช สงขลา ตรัง
ภูเก็ต และ ปัตตานี

กรุงเทพฯ เป็นเมืองหลวง ของประเทศไทย ตั้งแต่พ.ศ.
๒๓๒๘ (ค.ศ. ๑๗๘๑) ตั้งอยู่บนฝั่งตะวันออกของแม่น้ำ
เจ้าพระยา เมืองสำคัญ ของประเทศนอกจากกรุงเทพฯ คือ
อยุธยา ตั้งอยู่เหนือกรุงเทพฯ ตามฝั่ง แม่น้ำเจ้าพระยา
พิษณุโลก ลำปาง และเชียงใหม่ เป็นเมืองใหญ่ ทาง
ภาคเหนือ ทางภาคใต้ มี เมืองใหญ่ หลายเมืองเช่น
เพชรบุรี นครปฐม ราชบุรี สุราษฎร์ นครศรีธรรมราช
สงขลา ตรัง ภูเก็ต และ ปัตตานี

มีรถหลายชนิดที่ใช้กันในประเทศไทย เช่น รถยนต์ รถไฟ รถราง รถจักรยาน รถจักรยานสามล้อ และรถเล็กเป็นต้น เด็กๆและนักเรียนชอบใช้รถจักรยาน สำหรับขี่ไปเที่ยวและขี่ไปโรงเรียน รถจักรยานสามล้อและรถเล็กใช้สำหรับการโดยสารในระยะใกล้ๆ เพราะว่าต้องใช้แรงคน รถยนต์และรถรางใช้สำหรับการโดยสารทั้งในระยะใกล้และระยะไกล และใช้สำหรับการขนส่งของด้วย ส่วนรถไฟนั้นใช้สำหรับการโดยสารและการขนส่งระหว่างเมืองต่างๆ รถไฟในประเทศไทยสะอาดและสบายมาก ความยาวของทางรถไฟในประเทศไทย ประมาณ ๒๐๐๐ ไมล์ หรือ ๓๒๐๐ กิโลเมตรเศษ.

สิ่งทอทายเหิดที่มี...ในประเทศไทย
เช่น รถยนต์ รถราง รถไฟ รถจักรยาน รถ
จักรยานสามล้อ และรถเก๋งวิ่งยนต์ เต๋งๆและ
นักเรียนของมีรถจักรยานสำหรับใช้ไปมาเที่ยวและ...
ไปเรียนเรียน รถจักรยานสามล้อและรถ...
สำหรับการโดยสารในพระนครๆ , พระ...
ใช้แรงคน รถยนต์และรถรางใช้สำหรับการ
โดยสารทั้งในพระนครและ...ไกว และใช้สำ-
หรับการหนร่บของด้วย ส่วนรถไฟนั้นใช้สำหรับ
การโดยสารและการหนร่บระหว่างเมืองต่างๆ รถ
ไฟในประเทศไทยขณะนี้มี ทางยาว ความ
ยาวของทางรถไฟในประเทศไทยประมาณ ๖๐๐๐
ในอักษิ ทายๆ มีโดยสาร เศร.

SAMPLES OF THAI PRINTING

Samples of a variety of Thai printing styles in an assortment of sizes are given on pages 110-115. Those on pages 110-112 are used in newspaper headlines, and those on pages 111-112 are also often used for titles of articles and for paragraph headings. Page 113 contains samples of dates in an assortment of type styles and sizes. Pages 114-115 show a few samples of attention-getting styles of type which are used as heading for special columns, feature articles, stories, advertisements, etc.

These samples of Thai printing can be made use of by the student in a number of ways. In the early stages of his study of the Thai writing system, the student can use pages 110-112 as an exercise in the identification of consonant symbols. All but the rarest consonants are illustrated on these three pages. When using this material for identification purposes, the student should merely identify the consonants, calling them by name, e.g. /cɔɔ caan/, /dɔɔ dèg/, etc. Later on he can use the same pages as a series of exercises in the identification of vowel symbols, tone marks, and typographical signs.

After he has learned the Thai numerals on pages 83-84, the student can use page 113 as a numeral identification exercise. Then since the same page contains examples of dates in both full and abbreviated form, the same page can be used as an exercise in reading dates after the section on dates (pages 99-100) has been studied.

When the student has finished working through all the rules of the Thai writing system, he can use the various pages of printing samples as a

series of reading exercises. Most of the words can
be found by looking them up in the THAI VOCABULARY.
Words not to be found there are listed below.

อนาคต	/ʔànaakhód, ʔa-/ the future (page 111)
เวียตนาม	/wîadnaam/ Vietnam, Vietnamese (111)
โนแมนส์แลนด์	/noomɛɛnlɛɛn/ No Man's Land (Eng.)(111)
ฮั้ว	/húa/ Hua (proper name) (111)
ขอบคุณ	/khɔ̀ɔbkhun/ to thank ..; thanks (112)
สหรัฐ	/sàhàrád, sa-/ federated states (here referring to the United States) (112)
ในด้าน	/naj dâan/ in the way (side) of (112)
โทริเซน	/thoorisen/ Thorisen (proper name)(112)
แง่	/ŋɛ̂ɛ/ angle, point (114)
เกาหลี	/kawlǐi/ Korea (115)

The printing styles illustrated on pp. 110-113
are sufficiently clear so that the student should
have no difficulty in identifying all of the symbols. Some of the styles on pp. 114-115, on the
other hand, are more difficult. A typewritten key
to the material on those two pages is therefore
given below.

Page 114	Page 115
จดหมาย	ภาพยนตร์ วันนี้
ใคร–อะไร–ที่ไหน	ขาวแผนกฝึกหัดครู
ใคร อะไร ที่ไหน	ปัญหาประจำวัน
ฟังว่า	เก็บ เล็กผสมน้อย
แง่คิด	ในเกาหลี
ทำกับข้าวไม่เป็น	ไทย

จด หมาย จาก กรุงเทพ ฯ

พุทธศาสนา ใน อินเดีย

วิทยาศาสตร์
ภาพข่าว
ป้องกันอาเชียตะวันออกเฉียงใต้

ข่าวสมาคม
บทบรรณาธิการ
การประชุม ๔ มหาอำนาจ
ตรวจราชการ
อนาคตมืดในเวียตนาม
เรื่องไม่เป็นเรื่อง
ช้าง และ การล่าช้าง
โนแมนส์แลนด์ในอินโดจีน
ฐานะของสตรีไทย
บริษัท บี.เอ็ล.ฮั้ว จำกัด

พม่าขอบคุณไทย

สหรัฐขอซื้อดีบุก จำนวน ๒๔๐๐ตัน

ห้ามพ่อค้าเบี้ยหนี้ ส่งสินค้าออกขาย

น้ำอาจจะท่วมใหญ่

เขมรขอให้มหาอำนาจรีบช่วยเหลือ

ทั้งในด้านอาวุธและทางเศรษฐกิจ

ผู้ว่าการจังหวัด เตือนตำรวจ

เครื่องไฟฟ้าใหม่ มาถึง ครบแล้ว

ครม. พิจารณาช่วยราษฎรชาวอิสาน

เนื่องจากฝนตกน้อยจนทำนาไม่ได้

สารบาญโฆษณา

ของประเทศอังกฤษ อเมริกา ฯลฯ

บริษัท โทรีเซน (กรุงเทพ ฯ) จำกัด

วันที่ ๑ กันยายน ๙๔
๙ พย. ๖ ธค. ๓ มค.

วันพฤหัสบดีที่ ๖ กันยายน ๒๔๙๔

๑ มิถุนายน ๒๔๙๗ ๒ กรกฎาคม ๒๔๙๗

วันอังคารที่ ๑๙ มกราคม พ.ศ. ๒๔๙๗

กุมภาพันธ์ ๒๔๙๔   เมษายน ๒๔๙๔

ประจำวันที่ ๓๑ ธันวาคม ๒๔๔๔

อังคารที่ ๓๐ ตุลาคม ๙๔

วันอาทิตย์ที่ ๑๔ พฤศจิกายน พ.ศ. ๒๔๖๗

วันที่ ๒ ต.ค. - ๖ พ.ย. พุทธศักราช ๒๔๔๔

วันศุกร์ ที่ ๒ กรกฎาคม พ.ศ. ๒๔๕๗

วันอังคารที่ ๒๐ พฤษภาคม ๒๔๕๕

ตั้งแต่ ๒๔ มีนาคม ถึง ๗ พฤษภาคม ๒๔๘๕ เวลา ๙.๐๐ - ๑๒.๐๐ น.

เมื่อวันที่ ๖ ธันวาคม ๒๔๘๘ เวลา ๑๖.๒๐ น.

จดหมาย

ใคร · อะไร · ที่ไหน

ใคร อะไร ที่ไหน

ฟังว่า

แง่คิด

ทำกับข้าว

ไม่เปน

ภาพยนตร์
วันนี้

ข่าวแผนกฝึกหัดครู

ปัญหาประจำวัน

เก็บเล็กผสมน้อย

ในเกาหลี

ไทย